DONE WITH DATING

DATING JUST GOT SERIOUS
CHARACTER CHART

Book One
Blind Date
Phoebe Rogers & Cory Reese

Book Two
A Single Date
Yani Maxwell & Drew Sizemore

Book Three
Date Me
Cat Preston & Jeremy Gavin

Book Four
One Date At A Time
Geeta Preston & Brook DiNardo

Book Five
Speed Date
Egypt Carrington & Declan McKinney

Book Six
Done With Dating
Renee Payne & Richard McKinney

Other Books By Jacki Kelly

THE SWEET ROAD SERIES

The Sweet Road Home

The Sweet Road To Love

The Sweet Road Back

DATING JUST GOT SERIOUS

Blind Date

One Date At A Time

Date Me

A Single Date

Speed Date

Dating Just Got Serious – Box Set

WOMEN'S FICTION

Packed and Ready To Go

Going Backwards

Chapter One

Renee Payne stood in her bedroom examining the emerald green maid-of-honor dress. She should have been happy for her friend. She should have wished her friend well. She should have run away while there was still time. Instead, she sealed the ceremonial dress inside the hanging clothes bag, bit her bottom lip, squared her shoulders and vowed to suppress her stunted emotions.

From the dresser she grabbed the bottle of tequila and tucked it in her carry-on bag. All the festivities would be easier to enjoy if she was half-way to numb. A lesson she'd learned from her father.

With a sigh she picked up the phone and dialed Egypt.

"Hey Renee, I'm so glad you called," Egypt didn't say hello first. The new Egypt was always so jovial it was becoming disgusting. "Is Richard there yet? You guys should be on the road. They're calling for a Nor'easter, maybe a foot of snow."

"No, he's not here yet. I'm all packed, so when he gets here we can leave." Renee glanced across the room at her packed bags. "Tell me again why I'm riding up with him. I don't like him. I even squashed my crush on him."

Egypt was quiet for a moment. "Are we going to have this conversation, again?"

"After what he did to you, I think Richard is a big ass. Why you want me to stick close to him all weekend is ridiculous. Just the thought of having to ride with him to New York made me pack a fifth of tequila. I should start drinking now so he won't rub me the wrong way. I'd hate to commit murder before your wedding. I'm sure the McKinney clan looks down on that kind of thing."

"You can't drink." Her voice was high and squeaky.

"Like hell I can't. Between the storm coming up the coast and Richard, I'm going to need something to keep me calm."

"Renee, listen to me." Egypt's voice was sharp. "Richard is a recovering alcoholic."

"Did you say alcoholic?" A picture of her father sprawled on the sofa stung her memory.

"He hasn't had a drink in months. That's why you're riding up here with him. The family thought he'd stay sober if someone kinda' stuck by his side all weekend. A distraction."

Renee gripped the phone tighter, pressing it closer to her ear. Egypt couldn't have said what she thought she heard.

"Now don't freak out."

"Too late, I'm already freaked out," she yelled. "You know how I feel about drunks. I don't want to be anywhere near him."

"Just get him here and I'll find someone else to stick by his side. We should be able to get someone to do it."

"Why are you being nice to that jerk? Because of him Declan almost dumped you. If he can't behave himself in public, let him keep his stuck-up-ass at home." Rage crawled up Renee's spine, spewing venom like confetti. Too bad Egypt wasn't there to witness her frustration. "Can't someone else be on alcoholic watch, like a professional or his sponsor?"

"Renee, please don't weasel out now. Nobody else wanted to do it and he practically passes by your front door on the way here. It's important to Declan, so it's important to me. Pleeeeeeze."

This was her opportunity to beg out of the wedding. But Renee wouldn't, no matter how much she wanted to. She made a promise and she had to keep it. She always kept her promises, even when she shouldn't. It was too late for her to become someone she'd read about in how-to-books, who knew how to say no.

"Please, Renee. You were always talking about how good-looking he was. I didn't think you'd mind."

"Yeah, but that was before you told me he was a drunk. You know what I went through with my father. I don't want to be within ten feet of a man with a passion for liquor over life."

"Ugh! This is so much…so much…" She was crying. Renee recognized the sound. She'd heard it often enough.

"Okay, I'll do it, but only until we arrive. After that someone else can be glued to him and you'll owe me big time. I'm not talking about treating me to dinner or some lame gift card." Renee's voice shook. She was always giving in to Egypt's requests, but this was the last time.

"Okay, okay, just tell me what you want and I'll do it."

"Find me a great guy like Declan." She wanted to pull the words back. No one was supposed to know.

"I thought you said—"

"Forget I said that. It was a joke."

"Just one more thing, Renee."

"Oh hell, what else do you want? To lay me open and pull out my heart?"

"Take the liquor out of your bag. It might tempt Richard. You know alcoholics can sniff out the stuff like bomb-sniffing police dogs." Egypt spoke softly as if she was trying to coax the tequila out of the carry-on.

"I don't need you to tell me about alcoholics. I have firsthand experience, remember?" The words came out hard. She could have been talking to her father.

"That's why I thought you'd help."

The intercom buzzed. "I think he's here. I'll see you tonight." Renee ended the call and ran to the living room to hit the speaker.

The doorman's voice boomed through the speaker. "There's a gentleman here, he says you're expecting him. A Richard McKinney."

"Let him up."

This was going to be a test. A big one. He was the best man to her maid-of-honor.

It was easy to ignore him when he only came up in conversation, but flesh and blood Richard for the whole weekend would be an endurance challenge.

All she had to do was remember he lived in a bottle of booze.

Renee hurried back to her bedroom and carried her bags to the door. She put the tequila on the kitchen counter and shoved a stack of magazines in her bag.

All she had to do was ride with him to Glen Cove. Five hours with Richard. Five hours sitting one foot apart in the car. Five hours of temptation to ignore. She was screwed.

By the time he rang the doorbell, she had her coat on and her purse in hand. She opened the door and stared up at his dark eyes. Too bad they were attached to him. His broad shoulders filled the doorframe. He looked exactly like he did one year ago at Egypt's engagement party. His black hair was a little longer, falling down to his collar, and his face wasn't clean-shaven, but on him it looked good, good, good. His eyes were the darkest black she'd ever seen. He was every bit of six feet tall. Compared to her short frame, he looked like a giant.

"You're late," she said to Richard.

"Well hello, mate. I see you're still as pleasant as ever. I've had a bugger of a day, too." The sober Richard was even better looking than the inebriated one.

Some woman would be happy to snatch him out of the bachelor pool, but if he started drinking again it wouldn't take long before they threw him back.

How could she be attracted to an alcoholic? She had no intention of rescuing a man who didn't want to be saved. Her mother's constant battle was example enough.

Renee had a strategy for dealing with flawed men. Recognize the problem, get away from it, don't look back, don't overthink it, and God forbid, don't try to fix him.

He stomped snow off his shiny black shoes before stepping into the condo. Snowflakes dusted his shoulders.

"I'm ready, if you can take the big bag, I can grab the little one." She gestured toward the hanging bag and the suitcase.

“We aren’t going anywhere tonight, love.” He removed his coat. “Not only is it snowing, its monkeys outside. I spun out three times just making it across town, there’s no way we can make it to the state line.” He hung his coat on the rack, sat down and crossed his legs.

“You can call me Renee. And what do you mean its monkeys outside?”

“Oh, yes. I really need to watch my British slang, don’t I? It’s bloody cold.”

She rushed to the sliding glass doors and pulled back the curtain. A blanket of white covered everything. Streetlights twinkled in the blizzard like beacons. Everything was still like a Christmas post card.

She needed to be on the road, not cooped up in the condo with Richard.

His essence filled the apartment and she resented him for it. The idea of being attracted to anyone who could be like her father was too much to imagine. Besides, she wasn’t his type. He liked his women tall, lean and blonde and the last time she looked in the mirror she wasn’t lean, or tall and a long way from blond.

“This can’t be happening. We have to leave now.” Without turning around she said, “So now what? What’s the plan?”

"It's snow. It's not a bloody nuclear attack. It doesn't require a plan. When the roads are clear, we'll head out. Maybe tomorrow, maybe the day after."

"You're not staying here." She focused on a streetlight and the snow dancing down the slender black pole. The longer she pretended he was the big bad wolf, the longer she could ignore the rumbling in her stomach.

She could feel his eyes on her. With a huff she jerked around and looked at him. "So you'll come back and pick me up in the morning?" Her words rushed together like runaway rapids.

He snickered, or maybe it was a sneer, it was hard to tell. "I'm not going anywhere." He slid down on the sofa, looking more comfortable than he should. "You don't mind if I take off my shoes do you?" He'd already kicked off one shoe, banging it against the table before it thumped to the floor, and the second one followed.

"I'm not comfortable with you staying here." The living room was big enough for five people to sleep over, as long as one of them wasn't Richard.

"Well, hon, I'm not going back outside tonight. So unless you can lift my arse off this sofa, I'm staying here. Of course, if you're inviting me into your bedroom, then I can carry you." He raised one brow, the left one.

"You know, you're not nearly as charming as you think. Believe it or not, I think I dislike you more than anyone I've ever met."

"I knew I was special to you." He removed his jacket and loosened several buttons on his white shirt. More of his chest was exposed than she wanted to see.

"Are you always so f***ing arrogant. You're the only one who thinks it's funny, you know?" Her voice was amazingly calm even though she was nearing the point where frustration broke her like a child in need of a nap.

"The answer is yes. Arrogance is my superpower." She heard him say just before she slammed the door.

She pulled her cell from her back pocket and called Egypt. "He wants to sleep on the sofa…our sofa…my sofa."

"What? Can you talk louder?" There was noise in the background. Probably one of the endless dinner parties that was now a part of Egypt's life.

She cupped her hand over her mouth. "We're snowed in and Richard wants to sleep on the sofa."

"Calm down. Let me think."

When did Egypt become the one with the answers? She was the scatterbrain.

"Here's what you do. The two of you can get on the road in the morning, first thing, and you should be here in time for the afternoon activities." She was serious.

"You're missing the point. I don't want him to sleep here. It's enough to ride with him for several hours. Now the shit keeps piling on like an unending train of torture."

"If he's on the sofa and you're in the bedroom, what can be the harm? Come on, Renee. It's just one night." She sounded like she wanted to get off the phone and on to something more important. Like her perfect life.

"Egypt, this is not my drama. It's yours. Now you want me to watch him in a confined space. Alone. In a car, I can keep an eye on him, but I won't be responsible for him through the night and all day tomorrow. It's just too much." She didn't care that her voice grew louder, or who heard, or that nobody cared.

"Renee, please. I've already got enough stress." The tension in her voice was sharp. "There are so many cousins and aunts and I can't remember all their names. And Declan's mom is asking me about flowers and bows and everything. Please, handle this. I'm counting on you."

"You win. Your situation sounds worse than mine. But you're racking up a mighty big debt."

"I've got to run. If I hide out in the bedroom, maybe everyone will leave me alone for a few minutes." Egypt hung up before Renee could say anything else.

Renee flopped on the bed. A quick glance at the clock and her heart did a hard thug. It was only six in the evening. It was going to be a long night.

"Don't get involved with him, Renee. Don't even look at him too long." She pushed aside a vision of her father stumbling down the stairs, sprawling on the sofa, staying there for days.

When she was young, she thought all fathers slept in the living room. Every day her dad came home from work, dropped on the sofa and demanded her mother deliver him a steady stream of beer. After each drink he slid lower until his head was on the sofa arm and his feet were on the other. By the time she started high school, the beer had turned into scotch, straight up.

Other fathers showed up for school events, but Clyde Payne slipped away from his family one drink at a time. Nothing they did or said was more important than the pleasure he found in his highball glass.

In the beginning her mother used to say, let's be thankful he's not a mean drunk. Back then he was a quiet drunk. It was as if the liquor rendered him speechless, with nothing to say to his family or the world.

Renee jumped up. "Shit. Shit. Shit." She rushed to the bedroom door. Richard was in the kitchen, his back to her, his hands trembling. He was inches from the tequila. She could almost feel the high-powered static between him and the bottle. It was as strong as the current coursing through her veins.

Chapter Two

For a moment she wanted to touch Richard's shoulder, maneuver him out of the kitchen, away from the trouble.

Her twelve-year-old self swatted her hand, switched off her emotions, and sealed off her heart. It hadn't worked on her Dad. She didn't need to try it on Richard. He was someone else's responsibility.

This was not what she bargained for. Resentment ran through her veins like a stampede of wild horses. This was another reason why she shouldn't have agreed to be Egypt's maid of honor. There was nothing honorable about her feelings right now. If Richard wanted to waste his life drifting in a stupor, then he was certainly entitled to do just that.

"Go ahead, open it." The taunt was riddled with sarcasm, just the way her mother spoke to her father on those late nights when he managed to make his way off the sofa to stumble into the kitchen pretending he wanted water.

Richard didn't turn around, but he stiffened. "You know?"

"Egypt told me."

"She shouldn't have. It's none of her business and it's none of yours, either. It's not as bad as any of them think." He shoved his hand into his suit pants and headed back to the sofa.

She followed him. "You know, that's what they all say."

"Who is all?" He sat in the same spot and intertwined his fingers behind his head.

"Drunks. Alcoholics. They all think it's one big joke and that it's something they can handle."

He faced her. "What are you, an expert?"

She wanted to sit on the comfortable sofa, but it was too close to him. She sat on the straight-back chair across the room instead. "Yeah. I guess I am an expert. Growing up with my father qualifies me."

He tilted his chin up. His eyes locked on her as if he was trying to determine how much truth was in her statement. "Don't think you know me. I've been here for less than an hour and I'm nothing like your father." His eyes were cold, threatening her to keep her distance.

"Look buddy, I don't care what you do with your life. It's yours to screw up. Suit yourself." She jumped up and started for the bedroom. "If you think I'm going to hide that bottle from you then you're mistaken. It's staying right there and if you drain it tonight, shame on you. See if I care."

"Are you always so evil? What the hell are you mad at the world for, anyway?"

His words stopped her. "You don't know me either. So don't assume you do. Maybe I have more right to be mad than you have for being a drunk."

"Well, it looks like we have something in common. We don't know each other and we don't like each other. Have I gotten the facts straight?"

She placed her hands on her hips. Agreeing with him would have given him a concession that she didn't want him to have. His tall, lanky frame looked much too comfortable stretched out on her sofa. She wanted to push him onto the floor.

"What time are we leaving in the morning?" she asked.

"Who knows? We'll see." His casualness fanned her anger.

"You are not making all the decisions. If the snow stops, we're leaving as soon as the sun comes up. Be ready."

"Or what, you'll leave me?"

"Don't push it, Richard. Egypt is looking for us to get there as soon as possible and we're going to do it. I made her a promise and I plan to keep it even if I have to drive myself."

He chuckled. "Woman, you are a piece of work."

"You're one to talk." Her words were as sharp as his.

"Since I walked through the door all you've done is complain. It's no wonder you're alone. You're miserable." He closed his eyes.

Anger clogged her throat. A bucket of nasty responses percolated in her head and was ready to spew his way, but that would only prove his point. "I'm alone because I chose to be. Regardless of popular belief, every woman doesn't need a man to feel complete."

"That's what every lonely woman says." He didn't open his eyes. He must have enjoyed picking at the one thing she didn't want anyone to know.

"So if what you're saying is true, where's the beautiful woman who should be glued to your arm?"

"Touché. You've got me there." She couldn't tell if the grin on his lips was mocking her or if he was being sincere. "I guess that makes us two miserable souls. Welcome to my world."

Storming out of the room would have been just as pitiful as trying to defend her choice to be single. It really wasn't a choice, but the universe certainly was trying to teach her something and she decided to listen. If the alcoholic cousin could see through her shield of indifference, then she wasn't hiding her disappointment of being alone half as well as she thought.

She closed the bedroom door and flopped on the bed. It was going to be a long night. She dialed Egypt's number.

"Hey," she said when her friend picked up. "I know you're busy and swamped, I just need you to talk me off the ledge."

"What is it? What happened?"

"He's just so damn arrogant. I'm trying not to go into the living room and douse him in my tequila." Renee removed her boots and kicked them under the bed.

"Why? Oh, this is not good. It's not good." She sounded like she was on the verge of tears.

"Don't worry. We'll leave first thing in the morning. Believe me. I want to get him out of here as soon as possible."

"But if you guys don't get here by three, you'll miss the ice skating event. And you know I need you. Everybody else is not coming until later. I feel like I'm being swallowed by McKinneys."

"You might as well get used to those feelings, you're marrying into it."

"I'm marrying Declan. We won't have to deal with the whole family every day. Besides, they're all very nice. It's just hard trying to remember which aunt is married to which uncle and whose kids belong to which Mom. I feel like I'm cramming for an exam." The stress of the event was getting to Egypt, her voice sounded higher pitched than usual.

"I'm sorry. I promised to be there to help you and now I'm not. We'll get on the road as soon as possible. I'll even try to keep Richard alcohol-free."

She ended the call and sat up on the edge of the bed. After a long sigh, she made her way back into the living room.

Richard was still sprawled on the sofa, with his eyes closed, much like her father used to. She doubled back and checked the bottle of tequila. It was still sealed.

"I didn't touch your precious liquor. You can stop worrying."

"I wasn't—"

"Yeah, you were. No need to lie. My feelings aren't hurt." He placed his forearm over his eyes.

"I thought I should come out here and keep you company." She sat on the loveseat opposite the sofa.

"No need to do that either. I'm just fine."

"Look, I'm trying to be nice."

"Too late."

"How about some music." She started to get up.

"No. I don't want to hear any of your American Hip Hop.

"Look, I'm trying, here. There's no need for you to be so snippy."

"Well stop it. I don't want to be entertained."

"Suit yourself." She unfolded her legs and walked in the kitchen.

She'd planned to eat on the way to New York. Her stomach was in violent disagreement with the absence of food since the plain bowl of corn flakes she'd eaten for breakfast. Now it was time for Plan B.

She opened the door on the refrigerator. The chicken piccata and linguine pasta from yesterday's dinner was the only thing tempting enough to consider.

She scraped the chicken and the congealed sauce from the plastic container into the frying pan. It was more than she could eat. She balanced the remains over the pan and contemplated cooking the rest for Richard. He certainly didn't deserve the meal, a jelly sandwich would be more appropriate, but that was the mean person embedded in her veins directing her behavior. She ignored the notion and placed all of the leftovers into the pan. An image of Egypt nodding with satisfaction popped in her head.

It didn't take long for the crisp scent of lemon to infiltrate the condo. From the kitchen she could hear Richard stirring. She peaked around the corner to see him sitting on the edge of the sofa.

He looked up and caught her attention. For a moment they stared and said nothing. "I hope there's enough for me. I didn't think I was hungry, but now—that smells delicious.

"There's enough. Can you get the plates?" She tilted her head to the cabinet behind her.

Richard hurried into the kitchen and without asking for directions, he managed to find the plates, the drawer with the eating utensils, and the napkins in the pantry. A man who knew his way around a kitchen without looking like he was trapped or asking nine hundred questions was refreshing. Her last boyfriend, Jonathan, only came near the kitchen when the meal was on the table. He had an aversion to anything he thought was woman's work, which was defined by his archaic father when Jonathon was too young to know women had been liberated.

Renee made a pitcher of lemonade using a mix, but she squeezed real lemons in it to give the allusion of homemade.

Richard waited until she sat down at the table before taking the seat in front of her. "You know I don't mind if you have wine or tequila for dinner. I'm a big boy and can handle it." He reached for the pitcher.

"No, this is probably for the best. I don't want to oversleep in the morning, and I love this stuff."

He filled her glass, too.

He cut a huge piece of chicken and stuck it in his mouth. Without meaning to, she held her breath and waited for him to say something about the meal. She expected something caustic, which would match everything else he'd said since arriving.

"This is pretty good." He nodded. "Are you the cook or should I save my compliments for the closest take out restaurant?"

He didn't seem to hold her sharp words against her. He was being quite the gentleman.

"I'm the cook. It's leftovers from yesterday, but it's the only food in the house. Since I'm in New

York for the rest of the week, I didn't go shopping. It was this or sandwiches."

"I make a mean peanut butter and jelly sandwich."

"How did you know that's almost what I was going to feed you for dinner?"

"I happen to like PB&J sandwiches. That would have been aces."

"Okay, then you can make them for us to take on the road tomorrow." She couldn't look at him. He was being nice, which meant he was plotting. When men were nice there was usually a reason. He'd never been sincerely nice.

"You're assuming we're going to be able to leave in the morning. At the very least, we'll be lucky to get out of here by midafternoon." He put another piece of chicken in his mouth and put the fork down.

She pushed away from the table. "The world can't come to a standstill because of a few feet of snow. You're being a wuss."

"Better a wuss than dead." He carried the plates to the sink. Without being asked, he started rinsing the plates and placing them in the dishwasher. "Don't you have a television? I want to check the forecast."

Her chest tightened. "I have one in my bedroom and Egypt had one in her bedroom, but she took everything with her when she moved in with Declan."

He dried his hands on a paper towel, then dropped it in the trash.

"Where are you going?" She crooked her neck to see where he was going.

"To your bedroom." He kept walking.

"Wait a minute." She jumped up, rushing behind him. "You can't just go into my bedroom."

"Have you lost the plot? Why not?" He didn't stop. His British slang made her objection sound childish.

"It's my private space." She jumped in front of him. "I…I…"

"I promise not to look at your frilly things. I only want to see the forecast. Either we look at the weather and make some plans, or we can sit on our hands and hope. Is that what you'd prefer to do?"

Standing next to him, she felt inadequate. She was supposed to be the one in charge of the situation. He was the rummy who needed her help to get from Point A to Point B.

She allowed him in the room. "Just don't get any ideas."

He smiled at her, but it wasn't sincere. "I wouldn't dare."

Chapter Three

He sat at the foot of the bed and she sat close to the headboard. She aimed the remote at the television and turned it on. If he had to watch the television, she had to control the remote.

"Can you turn to a local network? We're only interested in what's happening here in D.C."

"I don't need you to tell me what to do." She changed the channel to WTTG.

He didn't look like the typical alcoholic. Everything about him was impeccable. His hair was trimmed, his shirt was ironed and crisp, and he didn't smell like a mix of cologne and whiskey.

She pretended to listen to the reporter who thought standing in the blizzard would prove to everyone how nasty it was outside, but she didn't hear anything. She couldn't get past Richard in her bedroom. On her bed. The last time there was a man in her bedroom was two years ago. Not that Richard counted, since he wasn't trying to get in her pants.

"It's supposed to snow through the night. They aren't predicting it to taper off until noon." He didn't look at her.

"Why are you all alone? You're a nice-looking man. Your attitude is a little funky. I mean with the whole nose in the air superiority thing you do, but there should be some woman who's willing to overlook that." She picked up a magazine and flipped through the pages.

He glanced over his shoulder. She braced for him to say something just as biting. Since he walked through the door, they'd been trading barbs, which was a continuation of all of their previous meetings.

"You ask a lot of questions. I really don't understand your low opinion of me." There was no resentment in his voice. He stared at her for a moment and then turned back to the television.

She sat up on her knees in the middle of the bed. "You tried to break up Egypt and Declan. You didn't think she was good enough to marry into your family." Her voice was shrill. "How can you pretend you don't understand? Egypt might be able to forgive you, but I'm certain I never will." She crossed her arms over her chest like an angry kid. She had an unforgiving streak that was as wide as it was deep. Every member of her family could testify to it. Growing up the way she did, she had no choice.

He shrugged. "Just goes to show you how bad my judgment is, doesn't it. I'll make sure I thank your dear friend for being so understanding."

He continued to focus on the television. Nothing had changed.

The snow was still coming down.

It was still cold.

And they were still stuck.

"You didn't answer my question. Why don't you have a date for the wedding? Since we can't get on the road, I figure I might as well ask everything I want to know about you. There is nowhere for you to run off to."

"Let's see." He adjusted his position on the foot of the bed but continued to look at the television. One of his legs swung back and forth with a steady rhythm. "Relationships are far too complicated. With the compromising and the talking and the sharing. I really believe they're highly overrated. I don't get love. I don't understand how it's supposed to work between a man and a woman. Forever is a joke and everyone seems quite content to buy into the hype, but not me."

"The alternative is being alone. Forever."

"Yes. That's the life for me."

It was easier to talk to him while he focused on the weather. His undivided attention would have only made her nervous, or tongue-tied or worse, vulnerable.

"If you're so happy with your life, why do you drink?"

Her question hung between them for several moments. His leg went still. It was the only indication he'd heard her. The sound of the weather forecast faded into a monotone drone filling the space between them.

"I haven't had a drink in a year."

"What? And for that you want a cookie, an award? How about a trophy?"

"I was simply answering your question," he said.

She snapped her finger. "All of you alcoholics are alike. You didn't answer my question. I asked why you drink. Not when was your last one. Don't forget, I know all the little tricks you guys try."

"Believe me, I have no interest in trying to trick you. This is just my usual response. I'm not used to anyone being quite so nosy. Let me ask you a few questions." He flipped over on the bed, looking directly at her now. "When was the last time you got laid?"

"Go to hell, Richard." She pushed back against the headboard, trying to put as much room between them as possible.

"Just as I thought. You don't like it so much when I get personal do you? But let me ask it another way. When was your last serious relationship?"

Renee glanced at her fingers. The short jagged nails needed attention. How could she be in a fabulous wedding with claws that looked like she'd been climbing mountains? If she didn't make it to Glen Cove by tomorrow, she'd have to keep them hidden.

“Is our conversation over?” Richard asked.

“It’s been three years. He treated me lousy and I put up with it. He forgot my birthday, and I put up with it. When he started cheating, I refused to put up with it. There were a few other guys since then, but after a date or two, it was obvious I was wasting my time.”

“Fair enough. Now I guess it’s my turn. While I might not have been proud of my behavior sometimes when I drank, I never had a problem.” He sat up.

“You’re still in denial.” She uncrossed her legs. The bedroom wasn’t a good place to have this conversation. “Maybe we should go back into the living room.”

“You don’t believe me, do you? I didn’t drink every day. I didn’t need to drink every day. And I didn’t get sick if I went a day or two with no booze. I guess I was a binge drinker. Once I had one, I had ten. And the more I drank, the uglier my behavior.” He stared at her. The shield he seemed so intent on keeping between them disappeared. “To make everyone happy, I said I’d give it up.”

“That wasn’t so bad, was it?”

“Don’t go patting yourself on the back because of my revelation. I did all the work on my problems, months ago.” The features on his face softened. Not enough to reveal a smile, but just enough to make him a little more human.

"I think we're straight on the weather. Why don't you go back into the living room and get some sleep?" She stood and inched toward the door.

"I'm not sleeping on that awful sofa. We're both adults, I'll sleep here at the foot of the bed. And you don't need to worry. I promise I won't make a move on you."

She'd heard those exact words before. This was the only time they sounded insulting. She grabbed her pillow, a hand full of her favorite magazines and marched into the living room.

Chapter Four

Renee opened her eyes. The sun wasn't up yet. She hated sleeping fully clothed, it always left her stiff. She inched into her bedroom. Richard was still asleep on the foot of the bed with the remote in his hand. He hadn't made a move all night, just as he'd promised. The television was still on. At least it wasn't the weather channel. Sometime during the night he must have changed it.

She ran her fingers through her hair, making sure she didn't look like a witch. She peered out the window, trying to be as quiet as possible.

With the pre-dawn light it was hard to tell if it was still snowing. She had to squint but she was able to see fine flakes continue to fall. From the window she was also able to see a thin band of black top. Her heart began to race.

She shook Richard's leg. "Wake up. I think we can get on the road. The snow has lightened up."

He was slow to stir. "Richard, come on. Did you hear me?"

"What is the forecaster saying?"

"Forget that." She pulled the remote from his hand and turned off the television. "We're getting on the road. We'll drive slow and take our time. I'm going to take a quick shower. I'll be ready in twenty minutes."

He sat up. His hair stuck up in places, making him look more like Tweety Bird than the handsome hunk who came through her door less than twelve hours ago. Finally she had an advantage over him. At least he wasn't gorgeous every minute of every day. She hurried out of the room. It would take more than bed head to make her feel comfortable with him.

There were times when she thought she had enough confidence to conquer the world. At other times, doubt coated her with a film so thick she couldn't escape the suffocating stench. It was all about her self-esteem, or lack of it. When she wasn't going full out to please a man, she wore a coat of armor so thick no man could penetrate it. The rough exterior she showed Richard suited her fine. He wouldn't try to get close to her. She'd use his shortcomings as a reminder of why she'd rather be alone on those lonely evenings when she only had her magazines to keep her company.

If he knew the full history of her background, he probably would have slept in his car last night. Her whole family was marked in some way by the behavior of their father. No one would believe one man could cause so much destruction by sitting on a sofa with a glass in his right hand. From anyone standing on the outside, her family looked normal, but the moment they stepped through their closed doors, the three ring circus started.

She showered and dressed faster than she'd ever done before. The size of the condo was much too small for all the emotion filling up in her. The jeans she slipped on probably wouldn't pass muster once they arrived in Glen Cove, but they were the only pants that worked with the boots she decided to wear. She grabbed her purse and rushed out of the bedroom. The living room was empty. She spun around, taking in the open apartment. His coat was still on the rack, so he couldn't have gone far in this storm.

"Good morning." His voice startled her. He came out of Egypt's old room, wearing only jeans. His chest was bare and so were his feet. His hair was wet and hung in soft waves around his face. "I decided to take a shower, too."

She looked away, ignoring her body's reaction to the sight of his bare chest. Her libido picked an odd time to wake up. "I wasn't sure where you were. Uh…Uh…maybe you should finish getting dressed so we can go."

"Okay, why don't you pack up the sandwiches I made?" He pointed to the kitchen table. "Peanut butter and jelly, just like I promised."

"How did you have time to make them? I didn't really think you—"

"It's nothing. I wanted to keep my word." He turned towards Egypt's room, exposing a massive tattoo on his left shoulder. The tat didn't fit with the Royal Family image that he portrayed. She couldn't make out the design, but she was willing to bet it was a family crest.

He disappeared and she wrapped the sandwiches. The vision of his bare chest invaded her thoughts. Good-looking men were common enough. Her issue was finding good men. It would take more than a few cheap sandwiches for her barometer of him to move. She pulled her cell phone from her purse and dialed Egypt.

"We're going to be leaving in a few minutes," she said when Egypt picked up. "We should be there by noon."

"Thank, God. I was beginning to worry." Egypt's relief was deafening. "How did it go last night?"

"Fine. Except he slept in the bed with me and this morning he made sandwiches," whispered Renee.

"What did you say? You slept with him?"

"It's not what you think. I'll tell you about it when I get there," Renee said.

"And what's that about sandwiches?"

"Richard made sandwiches while I was in the shower."

"Why are you whispering?"

"I don't want him to hear me talking about him. They aren't anything fancy, but I…I…"

"He's just trying to be nice, Renee. Don't over think it. Just get here. We're going snow mobiling later today and I want someone here that's got my back. I need my posse. I don't know why all of these people are so excited about snow. When I was growing up we went outside, made a snow man then came inside and drank hot chocolate."

"What about Declan's sister Maxi? You said she was cool."

"Yeah, but she was raised by the same people as Declan, so she's as gung-ho as the rest of them. And because of the weather everyone is arriving later than they originally planned. Look, I've gotta go now. I need to make sure I blow my hair out and put on my makeup before breakfast. Bye."

"I'm not so sure we should try the road so early, but I can tell fighting you on this will be fruitless." Richard came into the kitchen, his tight Henley was only marginally better than his bare chest. She blinked several times, pushing the traitorous thoughts aside.

One poor sandwich got a good thumb-sized dent from the pressure she exerted while placing it in the bag.

Richard made two trips to get the luggage to the car before the two of them locked up the condo together. A narrow path from the front door to the parking lot had been cleared, exposing a twenty-four inch strip of concrete. She followed behind him as they made their way to the car, which he'd already cleared off. He held the door for her and closed it once she was buckled in.

"Are you ready?" he asked once he put the car in reverse. "When we get on the Beltway I think we'll be okay."

Renee sat up straight to see over the dash of the big SUV. The goal was to help him. Two pairs of eyes had to be better than one. The city streets were barely passable. Blacktop was only visible in a few spots. In other places snow still caked the roads. They passed two men trying to push a car out of a snow bank. The right thing would have been to wait for the sun to come up. But Renee needed the distraction of other people, something she couldn't get in the condo.

"Are you okay, Love?" Richard gave her a quick glance.

She nodded.

"You're awfully quiet and I think you're going to pierce a hole in the arm- rest. Why don't you talk to me, it'll take our minds off the road. Ask me one of your famous questions."

"Okay, okay." She swallowed. "Have you ever been diagnosed with multiple personalities? I've been trying to figure you out and I'm stumped."

"What kind of question is that? No. I haven't. Maybe we should remain silent."

"I wasn't being mean. It's just you've been fairly nice since dinner last night. I haven't seen the jerky side of you."

His face relaxed into what was the closest thing to a smile. "Good save."

In the early morning hour, traffic was lighter than normal for a workday. Most people with good sense stayed at home as advised by government officials. Several streets had a slick sheen. Richard drove well under the speed limit. At their current rate, they wouldn't arrive in Nassau County until after lunch.

"Do you have any questions for me?" Renee asked.

"Unlike you Americans, I don't have the need to pry into the bloody private lives of others. I figure if you want me to know something, you'll tell me." He kept his eyes on the road.

"Then how do you ever get to know someone? It's called a conversation, it's not a test."

Richard's face dropped. The car jerked and began a slow slide sideways. Time stopped as they glided toward oncoming traffic. Everything happened in stages. Renee opened her mouth to scream, but nothing came out. With the skill of an Indy racecar driver Richard took his foot off the brake and twisted the steering wheel. Renee closed her eyes. Richard might have been in control, but she couldn't watch as the cars in the opposite lane bore down on them.

The car stopped as quickly as it had begun to slide. Renee opened her eyes to see they were just short of oncoming traffic, but they were facing in the opposite direction. Her heart pounded with such force she thought it would come through her chest.

"Oh my God." She mouthed the words, too afraid to speak them aloud.

Richard eased the car around. "It's okay," he said, placing his hand on her thigh. Even through her wool coat, his touch was assuring. "Are you alright?"

"No. I don't think so. I hate snow. Maybe we should go back. Maybe Egypt will understand," her voice wobbled.

"We're closer to the beltway now than we are to your place. We'll be fine." He sounded so sure. So confident. In all the years she grew up with her father, not once did he say anything with enough assurance to make her feel safe.

"Can we get there in one piece?"

"I'll take good care of you. You have my word."

It took twenty minutes longer than usual, but when they reached the beltway there was no snow on the road. The light flurries had tapered off, alleviating the driving tension. Her stomach was still as tight as a knot and her chest ached. But Renee was certain it was caused by more than the weather.

Chapter Five

Renee sensed they were close to their destination because the houses grew larger and further apart. Making the adjustment to this lifestyle wouldn't be hard for Egypt, her family was considered African American royalty in their small tight circle where they attended lavish parties and bought all the latest fads and trends. But for Renee, her pressure mounted as the miles in front of them decreased. She rubbed her palms on her jeans, hoping Cat, Yani, Phoebe, and Geeta had already arrived. The more people she knew the more comfortable she'd be.

"I don't think you've said ten words in the last ten miles. A new a record for you, I'm sure." There was laughter in Richard's voice.

She took a deep breath, letting it out slowly. "I'm excited for Egypt. I really am. But I have to admit, I'm not looking forward to all the stuff going on this weekend. This whole family thing makes me uncomfortable."

"Why do you care? You're not marrying into the family. You have nothing to worry about. We only eat our own." He turned onto a narrow drive and slowed down.

"My job this weekend—and I guess I chose to accept it—besides helping Egypt, is to keep an eye on you. History tells me that's a daunting task. I feel like everyone is depending on me to do something none of them wanted to do. And I get the distinct impression you don't want me hanging around you either."

"I don't need a babysitter. If you're worrying about me, stop." There was an edge in his voice she hadn't heard since the day before.

"I didn't mean to upset you. And no one asked me to babysit. They just thought if you had someone you could count on you'd be less stressed during all the celebrations." She hoped her words assuaged him. "You and I have more in common than you imagine. And I'm not talking about the drinking thing. You seem to be the black sheep of your family and I've worn those shoes before."

He gave her a quirky look she couldn't interpret. She wasn't sure if it meant that her words had worked or if it was a dismissal, but he turned into a narrow lane and she lost the conversation thread. There was a line of bare trees on each side of the drive. The surroundings channeled the long ago essence of a southern plantation more than a modern day estate. Renee half expected to see horses roaming in the pasture, instead she saw an open field being used as a small parking lot with over thirty cars, in all makes and models.

"It looks like everyone has arrived." Richard pulled behind a black SUV and shut off the engine. "While you're keeping me company from the nearest bottle of booze, I'll try to keep you company from the quick-tongued McKinneys. And just so you know, I'm not the black sheep of the family. My father holds that title and he hasn't relinquished it yet." His eyes darkened. There was pain in them. She knew that look and she knew the feeling even better. How many times had she wanted to punch her father for being such a miserable person and trying to drag his whole family down with him?

Richard walked around to her side of the car. They were parked in a field a few yards from the house and the snow was at least a foot deep.

Renee took a breath as if she was facing a firing squad and then asked, "Can we call a truce for now? I've got my own issues to deal with this weekend, so I won't have time to handle yours, too." She balanced on Richard's arm until she gained her footing. After everything they'd been through so far, it would have been so easy imagining they were a couple and that he cared about her. But unlike him, she couldn't hide from reality.

"You've got a deal," he said. "I'll have someone come back for our bags." He led her to the shoveled walk leading to the house. His hand around her waist kept her from falling.

The white brick house was as beautiful as it was big. The huge two-story columns studding the porch made it majestic and looking as if it was a set prop straight off a movie set. The second floor veranda wasn't quite as big as the one below it, but the wrought iron enclosure gave it an air of sophistication. A quick scan of the house revealed at least five wings, several of them appeared to be added after the original building. All she had to do was find one to get lost in.

"This place is huge. It's so beautiful." She couldn't help gushing.

"It belongs to Declan's father. I'm sure he'll inherit it one day."

Before they reached the front door, Egypt opened it and came running out. She wore a pair of shearling boots, but no coat. "It's about time you guys got here. Everyone has been waiting on you."

"We had some snow to contend with," Richard climbed the brick stairs and kissed Egypt on the cheek. He turned and extended his hand to help Renee, even though an abundance of salt had taken care of any ice that might have formed on the stairs.

Renee threw her arms around Egypt and held her tight. "Girl, I've got things to tell you," she whispered in Renee's ear.

"I heard that," Richard said.

Renee laughed away his comment.

The journey from Washington to Glen Cove felt like it had taken an eternity. At least now there were plenty of people to help buffer the blooming tension between her and Richard. He kept doing nice stuff. The kind of stuff boyfriends did for girlfriends. If he noticed the shift in their relationship, nothing about his disposition gave him away.

"Let's get inside and get warm. After lunch we're going out to play in the snow." Egypt herded them toward the door.

"Judging from the sarcasm in your voice, you're not fond of the afternoon activity," said Richard.

"You guessed right. I think I would have been a lot happier if we'd had the wedding on a nice island like Tahiti. I'm fonder of bikinis than I am of boots."

"Aren't we all?" Richard stepped aside to allow them to enter the house ahead of him.

Renee made a mental note not to look like a child in a candy store. Everything was so beautiful she wanted to move from one piece of furniture to another and run her fingers along the antique lines. The console in the foyer was a beautiful old piece of furniture. It could have occupied the cover of any magazine by itself.

In the distance, the murmurs of conversations could be heard. The noise level grew louder as they made their way through the house. So did the voices in Renee's head. She never wanted all this hoopla for her wedding. The idea of getting married one day was growing more foreign. The scars from her past liked to pop up at the worst time and sever any relationship that had half a chance of being a good one. She knew there were good men out there. Declan was one of them. All of her friends found good men. But she must have been awarded the same fate as her mother, but instead of being saddled with a lifetime of unhappiness, she'd take a lifetime of being alone instead.

They entered a sunny room encased in floor to ceiling windows. The glare from the snow made the room blindingly bright. There had to be fifty people, some were seated, others were standing in small clusters.

"Look who's here, everybody." Egypt made a flourish of escorting them into the room.

A swarm of McKinneys descended on Richard, swallowing him up as if he were a returning hero. The faces of Cat, Yani, Geeta, and Phoebe smiled at her, drawing her across the room like a bee to honey. With the help of her friends she could make it through the festivities. And with just a little luck, she could push thoughts of Richard out of her head, where they belonged.

Before the girls pulled Renee out of the room, she caught a glimpse of Richard. His eyes tried to convey a message. Egypt pulled her from the room before she could ascertain if he wanted her to stay.

Chapter Six

Renee was sure that left to herself, she would have gotten lost in the maze of hallways and stairs Egypt led them through. The other girls were full of giggles. To them this was a wonderful journey into the unknown. For Renee, her stomach was full of rocks, precisely because this was a journey full of unknowns.

What was Richard trying to say to her? Was the expression on his face about something specific or just another reaction from him about being here in general? She wanted to go back and ask, but Egypt's hold on her hand was tight.

They ended up in a large pink suite. Egypt's wedding dress draped over a form figure tucked into a corner of the room was the only indication that it was the room Egypt was staying in. Unless Egypt had changed more than Renee imagined, she hated pink, and all the lace and frills must be making her nuts.

Geeta and Cat were the last two to enter the bedroom, closing the door behind them. They looked more like sisters now than they ever had. Married life had brought them closer in several ways. Both wore their hair dark and natural. The loose curl pattern gave them a youthfulness that turned heads.

All six of them piled on and found a space on the king-size bed. All heads turned to Egypt.

"I have a question for you, Egypt," said Renee. "What do we get to do for you? Usually the bridesmaids and maid-of-honor throw the bachelorette party, but everything has been done."

Egypt placed her hands in her lap, as if she was preparing for a tough exam. "Declan and I talked about this. Instead of him and his crew going one way and all of us going another, we agreed we wanted to do something more inclusive. We want to build a life together, so we didn't see the need to start it off doing separate activities. But tomorrow we'll have the day together before the wedding. Just us."

"And you're sure you're okay with this? As your maid-of-honor, I want to do more."

"I'm just glad you all are here. Having my friends here is the only thing I wanted and you've given that to me." Egypt gave her a hug. "Now it's your turn to answer questions, Renee."

"Why are you guys staring at me?" Renee looked at each of them.

"What is going on with you and Richard? You guys slept together last night. I certainly didn't think you'd let him get anywhere near you." Egypt spoke before anyone else could say anything.

"No, we didn't sleep together…we were in the same bed, but only watching the weather forecast for a while. We were fully dressed. And afterwards, I slept on the sofa."

Egypt lifted her eyebrows. "That's pretty intimate for you. Whose idea was it?"

"It was his. But don't get it twisted. There was nothing going on. Nothing." She wanted to sound convincing, even if she had hoped to play out the fantasy of being with him that had been dancing in her head since she first met him. But, with ten pairs of eyes riveted on her and the combined intuition of over one hundred years, she didn't want to give them anything to feast on. She knew her friends well. When she first met Richard, they were relentless with their questions and innuendoes. When he came between Egypt and Declan, they all agreed she should give up her crush on him.

"Stop looking at me, ya'll. I am only doing what Egypt asked me to do." She shrugged her shoulders, trying not to give away her feelings. Making a fool of herself in the condo at home was one thing, doing it in front of a large audience was suicidal.

"I watched you two coming up the walk. The way he held on to you was more than just friendly. I've never seen him act so gentlemanly before. There was something going on," said Egypt.

"Love is in the air." Cat pretended to swoon.

"He was only making sure I didn't fall in the snow. We nearly had an accident on the way up here and he knew I was still a little shaky." Renee used her very best dismissive tone. As much as she wished there was some truth in Egypt's observation, there wasn't.

Egypt wrinkled her nose. "Before coming here I consulted my psychic."

A wave of sighs made it around the bedroom.

"Say what you want, but she was right about me and Declan. I think I've almost made him a believer. Anyway, she said there would be lots of love in the air for my wedding weekend," Egypt said with a conviction of certainty.

"She could have been talking about me. I'm pregnant." Yani dropped her hand to her abdomen, even though it was still flat.

"Squee!" Phoebe pulled Yani closer and hugged her. "That's wonderful."

Cat beamed. "Yani, congratulations. Now I won't be the only mother in our group. Someone else will understand when I have to ditch our girl's lunch for a play date."

"Yeah, but you've got two little ones. I'm playing catch up," said Yani.

"Just watch, pretty soon, we'll all be mothers, and instead of discussing dating and love, we'll be looking for the right pre-school and comparing notes on nannies."

"No, no, no." Egypt waved her hands. "I'm certain my psychic wasn't talking about babies. She was talking about grown-up love."

"How can you be so sure what she meant?" Geeta asked. "Brooks and I have been going through some challenges. I think we've worked them out. Maybe, she was seeing us in her cards."

Cat rubbed her sister's back. "The miscarriage?"

Geeta nodded. "The doctor said I'm young and healthy and we could try again as soon as we want. So we've already started."

A round of congratulations echoed in the bedroom.

"Okay, everybody," Renee said. "Let's assume there is a lot of love going on here this weekend. And a lot of lovemaking." She winked at Geeta. "But it's not Richard and me. I'm just trying to make sure Richard doesn't fall into a bottle of booze and ruin Egypt's big weekend. That's all it is."

There were a few skeptical nods.

"How do you think he's doing so far?" Egypt asked Renee.

"So far I think he's done well. But I saw the stocked bar downstairs." Renee shrugged. "If he's really got a problem, this weekend isn't going to be easy." She swallowed. "I still don't understand why you care about him. How could you forgive him?"

Egypt didn't respond right away. She appeared to choose her words with care. "If I hold a grudge against Richard, it doesn't hurt him. It would only hurt me and maybe Declan. In the beginning, I was mad at him. I even tried to think of ways to get revenge. But I realized it was weighing me down, changing who I was. And I figured it just wasn't worth it. Besides it was Declan's old girlfriend, Janie, who dug up the picture and tried to blackmail me. She's a hussy I keep at a distance." She faced Renee. "Look where I am now. Maybe his little stunt helped Declan to see how important I was to him."

"She's got a point," Phoebe said. "Sometimes you just have to let things go."

Renee snorted. "That's easy to say, but it can't be done in all instances."

A soft knock on the door interrupted Egypt. She jumped off the bed and opened the door.

"Can I come in?" a male voice asked.

"Not all the way. My dress is in the corner and you can't see it, sweetheart." The kiss she gave Declan made them all blush.

"Now we know the loving her psychic was referring to." Renee spoke low so that Egypt couldn't hear her.

Declan looked like a man happy with his station in life. He had the money, the elegant homes and a pretty bride-to-be. For him life couldn't be better.

"Ladies, are you ready to get outside? We only have a few more hours of daylight, so we need to get up the hill. We've rented additional snowmobiles, but there still isn't enough for everyone to have one. We'll have to share, but it's going to be fun."

"If there's a shortage, we can stay here," Renee called out.

"Oh, no. I've been planning this for months," said Declan. "We're meeting in the center hall in half an hour." The excitement in his voice matched the excitement gleaming in his eyes.

"I guess we're going to have to do this." Phoebe threw up her hands and climbed off the bed. "But somebody needs to tell him, black people don't do winter sports. Give us a call when it gets warmer."

A burst of laughter filled the room. "I know, right." Cat bounced off the bed and landed on her feet. "It might be fun. I'm going to change clothes. Any time I get away from the kids, I'll take it. Life must be lived to the fullest." Cat followed Phoebe toward the door.

"I've got an excuse." Yani rubbed her stomach. "I'll see if I can dig up some hot chocolate for your return."

The room emptied, leaving Egypt and Renee alone.

Egypt reached for her hand and held it. "Are you sure you're okay? You've got this look on your face that says otherwise."

Renee fingered a seam in the duvet. Egypt was being polite. She didn't need Renee crying on her shoulder or to hear her sad stories. But with all the emotion packed inside she couldn't keep everything pinned up. "Everyone is so excited and happy, I feel like an odd shoe. I know this sounds funny, but I'm Cinderella. I've been invited to the ball, but I don't have a date."

Egypt bit her bottom lip. "I'm sorry. I feel like I've inflicted this on you. I owe you big time," she paused. "You might manage to have fun while you're here. Declan and I have some fun stuff planned. It's going to be okay."

Renee patted Egypt's hand. "I'm fine. This weekend is going to be a blast."

They sat in silence for a moment.

"Come on, your room is just across the hall. Let's get this party started." Egypt jumped up.

Together they crossed the hall and Egypt opened the wide door.

"At least it's not pink." Renee said. "I could learn to like this. It's beautiful."

Egypt disappeared, leaving her to unpack and change. The room wasn't as elegantly appointed as Egypt's, but it was well above what she was used to. The soft yellow tones were soothing. There was a small balcony, but the only thing she could see from it was snow blanketing the shrubs and trees.

She dropped the curtain back in place and changed into the outerwear the sports store salesman had told her she needed for winter sports. She had no intention of getting behind the wheel of something powered and dashing across the snow, but she'd cheer on the others until her toes got too cold to stand it.

By the time she made it to the center hall, it was packed with people clad in vibrant colored parkas and boots that looked to thick too walk in. From her vantage point on the stairs, she scanned the crowd for Richard.

"There you are. I was beginning to think you weren't going to show," he said from behind her as he descended the stairs.

"Where did you come from?" she asked.

"Oh, this house has many staircases. When I didn't see you down here, I went around the other way looking for you."

"Were you disappointed, when you didn't find me?" she teased.

"Very." Richard reached for her hand. "We have to pair up and since you're doing such a good job of being my shadow, we might as well continue." He led her down the remaining stairs.

While the others teamed up, he stood so close she could feel the warmth emanating from his body. She didn't want to read something into his request, but her breathing escalated by the second. If she didn't calm down, she was going to embarrass herself and start hyperventilating.

When Egypt caught her eye, Renee looked away. The last thing she wanted was for Egypt to worry about her. Taking care of others was much easier than having to rely on someone to take care of her. She'd been doing it for so long, she was an expert at it.

"Uh…Uh…did you get settled in?" she asked Richard.

"Yes. Do your accommodations meet your expectations?" His dark eyes had flecks of gold and were so intense she almost didn't reply for fear of breaking the moment. It may have been the most perfect one they'd shared so far.

"I'm across the hall from Egypt."

"I know. I'm right next door to you."

She saw him smile for the first time. His words caressed her heart, leaving her short of breath.

"I'll have to remember that and try to keep the noise down." She turned away from him and tried not to blush.

He bent low, his lips brushed her ear. "Don't worry. I'm not a light sleeper."

She stood still, willing her body back under her control. It was well known that wedding hook-ups were only sophisticated booty calls. Anything Richard said and did had nothing to do with emotions. It was about hormones and nothing else.

She couldn't let a few nice words and gestures make her break the sacred vow she'd made to herself. Alcoholics didn't change. A twelve-step program couldn't mend a childhood of disappointment and the feeling of desertion she'd experienced while growing up. Her father had promised to change after every weekend bender, but he wasn't successful until a few years ago, long after the damage had been done.

Declan stood on the third step and clapped his hands. "Okay, grab your partner and let's head out. We've got a couple of good daylight hours left, so let's have some fun. We'll carpool to the top of the hill. Everybody should know who they're riding with."

"We're riding with Egypt and Declan." His lips brushed her ear again. He was doing it on purpose. Once was a lark, twice was a pattern. She didn't want to like it, but she'd be lying if she tried to deny it. A ball of excitement rolled through her body.

At lease twenty people marched out the door behind Declan. There were even a few kids who didn't look big enough to ride a bike. The snow was still soft and fluffy. The sounds of anticipatory giggles echoed off the bare trees.

The sporting goods salesman was right about thin insulated layers instead of bulky thick clothes. She was warmer than she'd expected. The troop made their way to the field where the cars were parked. Richard helped her into the back seat and climbed in beside her. Declan and Egypt sat in the front seat. Declan pulled around the other vehicles and slowly made his way back down the lane.

"Declan, we've got two novices with us, so we'll have to take it easy this time," Richard said.

"Does that mean you're going to take it easy on me too, cousin?" There was laughter in Declan's voice.

"Is this a family rivalry?" asked Renee.

"Yeah. I guess you can call it a rivalry," Richard said. "We've been challenging each other since we were three. Who can say the whole alphabet first? Who can learn how to solve a quadratic equation first? Who can move off the bunny ski slope first?"

"And who won?" Egypt turned to Declan for the answer.

"I won some. He won some," Richard answered before Declan could.

"He's being nice. He came in first way more than I did. I learned to do all those things, but not nearly as fast as him. Richard is driven. Once he sets his mind on something, there is hell to pay for anything that gets in his way," Declan said.

Renee expected to see satisfaction on Richard's face. Instead he stared straight ahead, his back teeth clenched. Did he also have something in his past that still hurt?

Declan brought the car to a stop. A whole set of gleaming snowmobiles graced the top of the hill.

"Whew! It looks like we've upgraded. When did you get these?" Richard stood back, taking in the shiny new machines. There wasn't a snowflake on any of them.

"We bought five new ones. The others are rented." As the others arrived, Declan waved the cars into a tidy row next to his SUV. It was obvious he'd done this before.

"Who cleaned them off?" Renee whispered to Egypt.

"Don't ask," she responded. "Their servants have servants."

Within minutes, Renee was seated on a contraption mounted on skis instead of wheels.

"Have you ever ridden a motorcycle?" Richard asked while he helped position her helmet.

"Never."

"Just hold me around the waist. I'll take care of you."

"You keep saying that."

"Haven't I done a good job so far? We got here in one piece, didn't we?" He snapped her strap into place.

He'd done exactly what he promised. She should have made him promise more. She should have asked for his word to keep her at arm's length. That he'd shoo her away like a pesky fly if she started to exercise poor judgment. She wasn't like the other women he dated. She was fragile, with a fault line running down the center of her heart. One sharp jar could cause damage that nothing, not even his words, could repair.

She didn't trust herself to speak, so she nodded.

"You mean you don't have anything to say. I didn't think you ever ran out of words. It's one of the things I like about you. Your sharp tongue is absolutely charming."

He didn't wait for her to respond. He hopped on the machine and turned the key igniting the engine.

Renee held him around the waist, like she was instructed. The last time she was this conflicted had to be when her mother invited her home to celebrate her parents fortieth wedding anniversary. She hadn't been home since she dragged in on Christmas Eve powered by guilt.

She couldn't muster the fortitude to do it again, three months later. She came up with a clever excuse that probably didn't fool anyone, but at least her parents stopped calling and asking. Her mother, she wanted to see. Her father, she didn't.

In this case, she wanted to be with Richard. Holding on to him felt exactly the way she dreamt it would. There were only two things wrong with her run-away thoughts. Richard hadn't shown any real interest in her and if he did, she'd have to reject him.

"You're going to have to hold on tighter. Even if we aren't racing, I'm not planning to cruise down this hill." He had to yell for her to hear over the roar of fifteen snowmobiles.

"How's this?"

"What are you afraid of, Love? I have never lost anyone on a moving vehicle before, so stop worrying and grab me like you want to make love to me."

A rush of heat enveloped her. Even in the freezing temperature, Renee wanted to unzip the parka and remove the helmet, but she was certain as difficult as it sounded, her face had to be bright red. All of her friends were looking for signs of romance and she refused to do anything foolish. She drew in a deep breath of the crisp air.

She was always doing this.

Imagining something that wasn't there.

Hoping for something that wouldn't be.

Wanting something she couldn't have.

With a new resolve, she wrapped her arms around Richard's waist, imitating the way Egypt held on to Declan. Declan's sister, Maxi held onto Yani's husband, Drew, as if they were a couple. If Yani knew Maxi would be clinging to her husband like static, she probably would have gotten permission from her doctor to participate.

The roar of fifteen snowmobiles drowned out all conversations. With a quick jerk they were the first heading down the mountain. Renee closed her eyes and tightened her hold. The ride was rough, bumping down the hill like they were riding over speed bumps at sixty miles an hour.

It wasn't until they had been on the machine for several minutes that she was able to open her eyes.

They wove through a cluster of bare oak trees and then along a ridge. Richard was as skilled with the snowmobile as he was with the car. She tucked her chin lower inside the scarf to keep it warm from the rushing wind.

This was the closest she'd ever been to Richard. A small part of her was happy she was behind him. This way she could smell him, not his cologne, but his real essence. She pressed her nose as close to his neck as the helmet allowed and whiffed him. It was like falling down a rabbit hole. She wanted more, but she only had the right to touch his waist. Desire took over her senses and wrung her like a child's toy. She was emotionally exhausted and they hadn't even kissed yet.

She maneuvered her head in just the right angle to brush her lips along his neck. It was a stupid thing to do, but everything in Glen Cove was off kilter, so she could kiss Richard, then wipe it from her mind and that's what she planned to do.

At the bottom of the hill, he stopped the snowmobile and waited for the others. He climbed off and removed his helmet. "Wasn't that fun?"

She was slow to remove her helmet. Part of her didn't want to meet his eyes, certain he'd see what was written all over her heart. The other part of her couldn't wait to look into his handsome face for any indication he felt a bit of something for her. It didn't have to be love, or even a strong like. She would have easily accepted the hot, desire or lust. The last thing she wanted from him was ambivalence.

"It wasn't bad. As a matter of fact, once I opened my eyes, I had a blast." She unsnapped her helmet and lifted it over her head.

"Is that right?" He walked around the snowmobile and stood so close she could see little white clouds made by his breath. He leaned close. She thought he was going to brush her ear again, but he cupped her chin with his gloved hand. "Is that why you kissed me?"

"What are you talking about? You're crazy." She turned away, stepping away from him to look up the hill, hoping to see others coming to her rescue.

He came up behind her. "I'm certain of what I felt. It was definitely a kiss. Or a peck. Yes, that's what we'll call it. A peck."

"Aren't you full of yourself?" She faced him. "I was just making sure I didn't go sailing into one of those snow banks. You could have gone a little slower." She was pleased with the indignation she was able to muster. Her father had been good at it, too. Pretending to be wounded when caught with his hand where it shouldn't be.

Chapter Seven

By the time they made it off the mountain Renee was exhausted and embarrassed. At least Richard had enough manners not to mention the kiss again, but new electricity connected them. Even though she couldn't articulate the difference, it was there. In the way he helped her back on the snowmobile. Their next ride down the slopes was slower, but with more sharp turns, causing her to lean into him more and hold him tighter.

"You enjoyed yourself, didn't you? The wind against your face, rushing down the mountain was different for you, wasn't it?" he asked as they trudged through the snow back to the estate.

"Yes. It was different for me. I'm an inside girl. Being outside in winter for an activity other than going to work is not something I normally do. But I do think that was a jerky thing you did the second time around." She kept her head down.

"What are you talking about? I was trying to give you a thrill. Anyone could give you an okay ride. I wanted to give you one to remember." He reached for her elbow when she almost slipped.

"Then you were successful. Except I thought the second time around you were more aggressive than you needed to be."

"Well, I did go faster than I needed. I liked having you at my mercy. It seems the only time anyone can get you to be submissive is when they take your control away." There was a smug look on his face, as if he'd discovered something new.

"I didn't know you were into that kind of thing." She knew she was blushing, but didn't try to hide it.

"There are so many things you don't know about me."

"I know all the important stuff," she said.

"Ah, but there's where you're wrong. All you really know about me is what others have told you. I can assure you, I'm much deeper and more complicated than you can imagine. And I'll warn you, stay clear of me. I've been known to self-destruct and take others along with me." There was no humor in his voice.

He should have told her that long before he picked her up in Washington. She'd gone too far down this road to double back now. Her feelings were exposed and the knot in her stomach was the caution sign that hurt and disappointment were closing in. "Thank you for the warning."

He held the door and allowed her to walk into the house ahead of him. After several hours outside in the biting cold, the warmth was welcoming.

"I'm going to lie down for a while. I'm exhausted," she said. "My bedroom is up these stairs and to the left, right? This house is huge and since we came in a different door, it's hard to keep track."

"Ma'am, here's something for you." A servant handed her a teal envelope, almost the same color as her maid-of-honor dress. She had several more envelopes in her hand and handed one to Richard, also.

"It's the notice for dinner tonight and the activities for tomorrow," Richard said. "Come on, I'll show you to your room."

She followed him up the stairs, paying attention to all the turns.

"Here you are." He stopped in front of the familiar door.

"Thank you." She tore open the envelope. A single card instructed her to be at dinner at seven. "Oh great. We have less than two hours before dinner. I wanted to take a long hot bath and a nap." She looked up at him. "And the list of activities for tomorrow is just as daunting."

"It's a McKinney tradition. Tonight, if you can't do both, it looks like you'll have to make a choice. I'm going to do both."

“How can you do both? There’s not enough time.”

“I’ll just take a short shower and a shorter nap. If you haven’t already noticed, the McKinneys have rituals. And they must be followed. You wouldn’t want to end up on their bad side, now would you?”

She couldn’t tell if he was joking or serious. “No. I guess not.”

He stood so close to her, she thought he might reveal a secret. “I didn’t think so. I’ll escort you down for dinner. I’ll knock just before seven.”

Before she could say anything, he walked away and entered his room. Richard spoke as if his family had a mysterious secret or a dark side that required watching.

She was bone-weary and for now would accept his advice. Inside, the suite was dark. From the bathroom, on the opposite side of the room, a nightlight glowed, giving the pale room a soothing quality. After the excitement of the day, Renee needed to power down and recapture the key moments. She was enjoying his company. Maybe more than she should. For sure, more than she was willing to admit. She smiled at her reflection in the mirror as she pinned her hair up.

In the bathroom, she pressed the stopper into the tub and filled it with water as hot as she could stand it. She stripped off the layers of clothes, leaving them in a messy heap on the tile floor and climbed into the sudsy water. The chill that had invaded every inch of her body melted away, one inch of skin at a time.

Tonight was the welcome dinner. Tomorrow was wedding prep day, hair, nails, facials and massages. Under any other circumstances, Renee would have been looking forward to spending a day with her closest friends. Instead, she couldn't escape the idea that in a minute she was going to sink her size seven shoe onto a land mine and the delicate balance of her everyday life was going to blow up. The feeling she had for Richard needed to stay buried.

Just once she'd like to have a happy, carefree life. One without the scars she carried from childhood. One that didn't leave her looking for the monster under the bed. She closed her eyes and rested her head on the back of the large tub.

Her whole life could have turned out different. Back then all she had to do was make a different choice. If she had just gone to bed a few minutes earlier, or forgotten her thirst until the morning, or heeded her sister's warning that their father was in a foul mood and to stay away from him, any one of those things would have been a sufficient fork in the road to change her whole life. But she had ventured out of the safe haven of her childhood bedroom that she shared with her younger sister, Rhonda. She crept down the stairs, envisioning a chocolate chip cookie to go with the glass of water.

She'd turned the corner of the living room at the moment her father struck her mother's face with such force she fell to the floor, landing on both her hands and knees. Renee froze, unable to move as her father landed two more solid punches to the side of her mother's face.

"Mom," Renee yelled rushing to her mother's side.

"Go back upstairs, now." Was the only thing her mother said, but her tone left no margin for discussion. Tears blurred Renee's vision as she backed out of the room and darted up the stairs. Her body shook so hard she couldn't close her mouth. She burrowed into her bed and closed her eyes tight to block out the image.

Her childhood innocence was stolen in a matter of seconds. Erased with the ease of a swipe across a blackboard. There were other nights, more violent nights when her mother couldn't keep her cries muted, when her suffering rang through the house like the wails of a thousand women. Even though she never saw her father hit her mother again, the bruises bore witness for her. No longer could her mother brush them aside by saying she'd bumped into the door, or hit her leg on the table.

The bath was only supposed to be fifteen minutes long, but the warm water refused to release her. Whenever the memory came back to her with such clarity, it held on to her with the strength of a vice grip.

Her heart raced, making her breathe harder. She sank lower in the tub until the pain of that horrifying recollection released her.

When she stepped out of the tub, the bedside clock let her know there was no time for a nap. She had forty minutes to do something with her wet hair, get dressed and do her make-up before Richard knocked for dinner.

Instead of letting her hair dry into natural curls the way she liked; she pulled the hair dryer from her bag and blew it straight. The dress she'd hung up earlier was almost wrinkle-free. The black wool pinstripe halter gown was simple, but elegant. This weekend was all about Egypt, there was no benefit in trying to impress anyone.

She applied her make-up with the precision of an artist. Standing in front of the full length mirror she was pleased with her appearance. There were no markings, no scars or shadows to remind her of the past. Her secrets were safe. Only to be shared with her sisters, whenever one of them got tripped up by life and wanted to understand why they were always being singled out.

There had to be a reason for those memories to resurface, here, now. It was a warning.

Just in case she'd forgotten how much damage alcohol could wreak.

Just in case she thought Richard was different.

When she thought she could escape from its hold on her heart, there were always those memories, just in case.

At exactly six fifty-five there was a knock on her door. She took a deep breath and opened it. Richard stood in the hall as flawless as new money. He wore a black suit, a blue shirt, and a red paisley tie. He must have done exactly as he promised, showered and napped, because he looked rested and refreshed.

With a silent sigh, Renee closed the bedroom door and joined him in the hall.

He tipped away from her. His eyes scanned her from head to toe. The attention made her uncomfortable.

"You look very beautiful." This time there was no doubt about his smile. "I'm honored to escort you to dinner." He stuck out his arm.

She wrapped her arm around his and they made their way down the hall.

"Well, you don't look too happy. Weren't you able to get at least some rest?" His shoulder brushed hers as they descended the stairs.

"Not even a wink," she said.

"Tsk, tsk, tsk. I should have come over. I'm sure I could have kept you on schedule."

"No. I don't think you could have helped. I've got a lot of things on my mind."

“We’ve had a long day. You woke me up at the crack of dawn, remember?”

“How can I forget? After dinner, I’m going to beg out and go back to my room.” They reached the last step and she dropped behind him. His presence was too much. It was time to pass him off to someone else.

Chapter Eight

Impersonating Cinderella hadn't been her intention, but dressed in the formal gown, in the pretty mansion, being escorted by the handsome man, was too close to the fairy tale she'd read as a child. Because underneath all the beauty was a tangle of lies and secrets. At midnight the whole evening could very well vanish into a fine mist.

Together, she and Richard entered the opulent dining room. The crystal chandeliers over the table were tastefully dimmed for dinner. The table was set with more china and stemware than Renee had seen before, even in the most upscale restaurant.

Beautiful velvet shaped hearts hung from the high ceiling. It was as if they'd walked into a Valentine's Day wonderland. A quick look around the room revealed every chair also had a bright red bow tied to look like a heart.

"I don't get the whole Valentine's Day theme," Richard said. "Doesn't it put too much pressure on the bride and groom to be more romantic, just to fill the illusion."

"Of course you wouldn't understand. You probably don't even believe in romantic love." Renee continued to survey the room for a familiar face.

"It happens to a lucky few. The others only pretend until they file for divorce or run off with their co-worker." His tone wasn't sharp, nor did he screw up his face like she noticed he did when talking about relationships.

"Let's hope for Declan's and Egypt's sake that they've found true love. Maybe then you'll be convinced."

He stopped in front of her. "And what about you, Renee? Have you ever been in love?"

She closed her eyes for a brief moment, scanning the long string of ex-boyfriends in her mind. Each one had some insurmountable obstacle they couldn't seem to get around. Or maybe she was the one with the issues. She opened her eyes. "No, I've never been in love. But I believe it exists. I've seen the way Declan looks at Egypt. I've watched Egypt walk around like she was on a cloud and I know they have something real."

"You poor thing. You've been manipulated by mainstream media and chick flicks. Maybe what Declan and Egypt have is real, but most people have a high dosage of lust. And believe me, sometimes, that's just as good."

"Are you going to be a downer for the whole weekend?" She narrowed her gaze on him.

"I'm just a realist." He reached for her hand and continued into the room. "Can I get you a drink?" He lifted a glass of champagne from a passing server.

"No." The words came out more forceful than she wanted. Several people turned to face them. "I mean…I…I—"

"Don't worry about me. I can take care of myself," he said. "Like I told you earlier, I don't need a babysitter." The playfulness in his tone was gone. The sharp set of his eyes warned her they'd stepped into a danger zone.

"I don't want a drink, Richard. And it has nothing to do with you." She lowered her voice. "I'm going over to talk with my friends." She left him standing in the middle of the room.

"What was that about?" Geeta asked when she approached.

"It was nothing."

"It sure didn't sound like nothing." Geeta's husband Brooks draped his arm over his wife's shoulders. Why did everyone have to be so demonstrative? They weren't getting ready to enter the ark. There was no need for everyone to pair up.

"Where are Yani and Drew? Aren't they coming down for dinner?" Renee scanned the room.

"She wasn't feeling well earlier. Instead of morning sickness, she has all day sickness. She said she's going to try to make it down." Cat offered. "I told her she'd better. I think Declan's sister is trying to put a move on Drew."

"She wouldn't." Geeta sounded as if the idea was preposterous. Maybe Richard was right. Maybe it was all about lust and not love.

"Let's just say I'm keeping an eye on her." Cat spun around, her detective work already begun.

The room grew hushed. Renee turned to see what was going on. Egypt and Declan were entering the room. There was no mistaking it. The two of them had something special. Together they could take on the world. Before Declan came along, Egypt fumbled through life. She seemed to be uncertain where she fit in. But now, there was a serenity about her. Her search was over.

Declan pulled Egypt into his arms and kissed her. If that wasn't love gleaming in his eyes, it was the next best thing. Renee's heart ached. She wanted the same thing. And knowing it existed in the world should have given her hope. Instead, her knees buckled.

The feeling of being alone ballooned. This was a special occasion and she wasn't sharing it with anyone. She could always turn to her sisters for understanding and occasional companionship, but when it came to being with someone on a deeper level she had no idea what it felt like. She was nearing thirty and had never been in love. The ache in her heart grew, consuming her with raw emotion. She ran from the room.

She found a bathroom and shut the door behind her. Without turning on the light, she stifled the tears that threatened to ruin the make-up she'd spent so much time applying.

"Get it together, girl," she whispered into the darkness. She balled up her fingers, making a tight fist. Everything was happening exactly the way she thought it would. There was only one and a half more days and then she could escape back to the privacy of her apartment. It took several deep breaths before she was able to push down the emotions.

She flipped on the light and flushed the toilet, making a good gesture to appear like everything was normal. She washed her hands. A close examination in the mirror and everything was fine. She opened the door.

Richard was just outside. "Is everything okay, love?"

"What are you doing here?"

"I saw you run out of the room. I'm just checking on you." He handed her a fluted glass. "This might make you feel better."

She shook her head. "I don't want a drink. But thank you. That was nice of you."

"It's ginger ale. According to my grandmother, it'll settle what ails you. That is of course if it's your stomach causing you a problem. I took a shot."

She accepted the glass and took a sip. The pull in her stomach had to be her emotions riding on the surface of her skin. It wasn't anything more than that. She'd probably have another very similar moment during the wedding toast and first dance.

"Shall we?" He stuck out his arm and nodded toward the dining room.

"Thank you." She accepted his arm, but pushed away any thoughts that they could be a couple.

Everyone was already seated when they walked into the dining room. Richard led her to the two empty chairs across the table from Egypt and Declan. He held the chair for her and helped her pull it closer to the table.

"Are you okay?" Egypt mouthed.

"Yes," she mouthed back with a smile. Only marginally. She put on her best fake smile and ate her salad. She'd be a bundle of fun just for Egypt.

There was a steady buzz of conversation around the table. With no direct question addressed to her, she was able to sit in her own thoughts and sort them out. Every situation had a bright side, all she needed to do was find this one and enjoy it. Richard had lost his abrasive edge, and even though she shouldn't, she was enjoying him. Everything would return to normal when she got back home.

"Before the entrée is served I'd like to make a toast to my beautiful wife to be." Declan held his champagne glass high and everyone followed.

Renee glanced at Richard. This had to be an uncomfortable moment for him.

"Don't worry, love. I've got ginger ale. You see it does cure lots of ailments." When Declan completed his toast, Richard drained his glass.

"Are either one of you getting cold feet?" Maxi asked as the entrée was placed on the table.

"Maxi, you are such a busybody. If we were, we certainly wouldn't tell you, now would we?" said Declan.

"I'm just curious. Spending the rest of your life with the same person seems impossible. I know mum and dad did, but that's a different generation. They didn't have as many distractions." She spoke fast now. Everyone was watching her.

"Maxi, aren't you too young to be so cynical?" Richard leaned forward and glanced down the table in Maxi's direction.

"Save your breath, Richard. I think Maxi is just trying to get a rise out of us," said Declan. To accentuate his position, he drew Egypt into his arms and gave her a deep kiss, putting an end to the conversation.

"I take it Maxi must have gotten her relationship philosophy from you," Renee said so low only Richard could hear.

"No. As a matter of fact she didn't. But the divorce rate in our family is higher than the national average. So I'm just doing society a favor and staying single. But when it comes to children and pets, I love them all. I'm really quite incredible with them."

"I know this isn't going to come out right, but on behalf of society, we thank you," she chuckled, but there was some truth in her words. She pushed her half-eaten meal away.

Admiration blazed in his eyes. He placed an elbow on the table and studied her. "You know, I'm used to women who bend to my way."

She mocked his movement by positioning her elbow on the table, too. "Your relationships must be very boring."

"It is. But I haven't been bored since this time last night." There was a glint in his eyes that said he wasn't joking, this wasn't just frivolous dinner conversation.

She put her hand in her lap. "Now we're done with dinner, what else is on the agenda for this evening? If I don't get some sleep, I'm going to put my head on the table and take a nap."

"Knackered are you?" He put his hand on her arm. "Are you sure that's what it is or are you gutted by all the sentiment in the air. Being single at a wedding is like being a sneaker at a formal."

Impressed with his insightfulness, she was almost speechless. "You're right. I'm happy for Egypt. Really I am. I don't want to dampen her big day, but I feel so left out. The longer I'm here the more the feeling spreads."

“I think I know just what you need. Let’s go.” He reached for her hand.

“We can’t leave.” Renee pulled her hand away. “Don’t we have to stay? We’re part of the bridal party.”

He leaned close to her ear. “After this there’s only more drinking and toasting and storytelling. More of the stuff that’ll make you want to run screaming from the room. If asked, you can tell everyone I was getting a bit stressed out and needed to get away from all the toasting and the cheers. My family thinks I’m a miserable soul and they’ll be glad you whisked me away.

“You’ve got yourself a deal.”

Several people milled about, so no one seemed to notice as they left the room. They were out of the dining room within seconds and back in the main hall. He ran ahead of her up the elegant staircase towards their bedrooms.

“What exactly do you have in mind?” She remained at the foot of the stairs, daring her heart to beat any faster. This was not going to happen. The two of them doing something alone did not sound like a good idea.

“Let’s change into something more comfortable.” He said over his shoulder and waved her up. “Did you bring a pair of jeans and a pair of sneakers?”

She was doing it again. Jumping to ridiculous conclusions. She closed the gap between them. "I have jeans but no sneakers. There's over a foot of snow outside. What good would sneakers do me?"

"You'll be surprised." He waited on the landing for her to reach him. "Put on a pair of flats and I'll tap on your door as soon as I'm changed." His eyes blazed. He looked excited.

"Do I need my coat?"

"No."

Maybe now they were going to do something she could enjoy. She charged into her room and shimmied out of the gown. He knocked on her door before she had her shoes on.

"Come on in. I'm almost ready," she yelled.

He was dressed in a pair of dark jeans and a plain black sweatshirt. His hair was combed back and everything about him looked refreshing.

She slipped on the ballerina flats and stood. "How do I look?"

"Perfect."

Instead of using the same staircase, he led her down a different one. This end of the house was quieter and the lights were dim. The murmured conversations faded even more as they descended another set of stairs.

"Are we going into a basement?" she asked.

"Shhh. Not so loud or we'll have company and I'd rather we be alone."

She nodded. Having him all to herself sounded wonderful.

"It's not a basement. We're going to the game room." He stopped and turned on a light in the room.

Bright fluorescent lighting illuminated shiny oak floors, revealing a four-lane bowling alley. Across the back of the room was a series of leather seating. With a flourish of his hand he ushered her in, stepping aside to let her go in front of him.

"This is awesome. Other than the size, it looks exactly like the ones I've seen on television."

"Have you ever bowled?" He began flicking switches and the whole room came to life.

"Never. But I'd rather be down here than upstairs dressed like a black Barbie." She sat down beside him.

"You look better than any doll ever could." He gave her an appreciative stare.

The compliment made her blush. Something she'd learned to control in college. For the first time since arriving in Glen Cove she was able to take a real breath, one that wasn't tangled in dread or fear.

"Since I can't play, I'll sit here and watch you," she said.

"Oh no. I'll teach you."

He beckoned her to the lane.

"Okay, but let me see your technique first." She took a tentative step closer to him.

"I'll show you how it's done twice. Then you'll have to give it a try."

He stood several feet behind the white line with the ball balanced on his hands. After a deep breath, he took several long strides. The ball hit the floor with a thud, then whirled down the center of the lane, striking the pins and taking them all down.

He repeated the action again.

"Come on it's your turn."

"We're playing for fun, right? Promise you won't tell anyone how awful I am."

"You have my word." He positioned her just beyond the white line and showed her how to balance an eight-pound ball on her fingers. He stood behind her. With one hand around her waist he used the other hand to show her how to swing her arm back. He was so close it was more of a sexual dance than a bowling lesson. She tried to focus on the technique, but his touch was too warm for her to concentrate. Earlier in the day she held on tight to him and it felt wonderful. Now he was holding on to her and his touch was dizzying.

He led her arm back and together they took two steps toward the white line. The heat from his body sent her temperature up. She closed her eyes and allowed her body to rest against his. The ball went straight into the gutter.

"Okay that wasn't too bad. But on the next ball, keep your eyes open," he said.

By the sixth frame she was able to take down seven pins. She threw her hands in the air. "This is fun."

"Slow down, Love. I'm beating the pants off you," he said from behind the desk.

"Only because I'm not trying to win." She strolled over to him and bumped her shoulder against his.

The amount of physical activity they'd had in one day exceeded all of her past dates. Not since phys-ed in college had she used so many muscles. Richard had a level of freshness she wasn't accustomed to. He was drawing her away from the protective shell she had enclosed around her life.

"I noticed some competition between you and Declan this morning. What is that about?" she asked.

He rested his cheek in his palm. For several seconds he stared without replying. "Either you're very perspective or I'm not doing a good job of managing my emotions." He chuckled, but it was dry. "It took me three years of therapy."

"I know the feeling. But it's good that now you're in touch with your triggers." Their eyes met and they broke into laughter at the same time. "What's going on with you two?"

"It's a family thing. We are always in competition for something. He has the company. He has the position. He has everything I want. I've lived my life in his shadow. Can you imagine what it's like to always be compared to someone who's perfect?"

"There isn't any perfection in my family, so I'd have to say no."

"My father was a screw up, so instead of inheriting his share of the company, he got nothing. So instead of working beside Declan, I work for him." He turned away from her. "But I don't want to talk about it. What's done is done." He stood, making his way to the lane.

Which made her feel better. After two games she hadn't been able to perfect her technique. But Richard was patient. He didn't even laugh when she sailed halfway down the lane with the ball still attached to her hand.

Three games later they both were exhausted and too giddy to care about the score. He turned off the lights and they walked side-by-side back up the darkened stairs to the second floor. Outside her bedroom door she leaned against the frame. "Thank you, that was fun," she said while trying to silence a yawn.

He responded by using his index finger and lifting her chin. He pressed his mouth over hers and any thoughts of resisting vanished.

Chapter Nine

His kiss was exactly the way she imagined. Warm. Sweet. Inviting. Her brain must have taken an unauthorized leave of absence, allowing her heart to run the show. Having him this close was emotional suicide. At the hair salon there was always a conversation about disastrous wedding flings. She didn't want to have a story to tell. They were much funnier to listen to, than to participate in.

He deepened the kiss and she accepted his tongue. Her hands dangled by her side. To put her arms around him would have been full submission, and she couldn't do that. He pulled her closer.

This was real.

This was good.

This was wrong.

She wasn't a hypocrite. One night stands had their place. There were a few in her past. All of them were forgettable.

He opened her bedroom door and moved inside. The way he extended his hand to her resembled a scene she'd seen in the movies. If she stepped over the threshold she was saying yes. She hesitated. There were bad boys and there were boys who were pure trouble. Richard was trouble. The kind she knew from the inside out. She wanted to ignore the primal draw to him. She wanted to do the right thing. But she couldn't pull away or resist the hypnotic connection between them. One weekend is all she needed. Just this one night and tomorrow she'd strap on her armor again.

"I understand if you don't want to. Are you up for it?" he said without dropping his hand.

He wouldn't understand. Unless he grew up in the modest house on Emerson Street with the rest of the Payne family he couldn't appreciate the whirlwind of emotions she filtered through each time she kissed a man. There was no way he could make sense of how she tortured herself because she wanted to sleep with him. "I want to. But…you…"

"There are probably a million reasons why we shouldn't do this. But I can think of two reasons why we should."

"Oh yeah. What are they?"

"I want you. And you want me." His lips didn't smile, but his eyes did.

"You are really full of yourself, aren't you? What makes you so sure I want you?"

He wrapped his hands around her waist and pulled her into the bedroom. "Because you kissed my neck on the slope today and I can't stop thinking about it."

She dropped her head. "Okay, I did kiss you." She looked up into his face. "I've always had this thing for you, ever since we met at the club almost two years ago. But, you didn't notice me and then I found out you were a jerk, and then…"

"That's enough talking." He kissed her. His passion was unmistakable. The sensation of his hands as he moved them over her body turned her insides to liquid. She ran her hands under his shirt. Touching his flesh without having to sneak turned up her desire ten points.

He pulled his shirt over his head, giving her easier access to him. This was the stuff she dreamed about. But reality was more sinfully delicious than anything she could have dreamt up.

He picked her up and carried her across the room. She wasn't a skinny girl, but he didn't wobble. His hold on her felt secure. She clung to his neck. With each step she planted a kiss on his shoulder.

"What is all this stuff on the bed?"

"My magazines." He tilted her and she kicked them onto the floor.

He placed her on the bed as if she were as delicate as a raw egg.

There was tightness in her heart. It was a warning. She'd made so many promises, vows, oaths about how she was going to conduct her life. The list of do's and don'ts was longer than her arms, but none of them mattered right now.

He lifted her shirt over her head to cup her breast. “From the moment we stepped into the bowling alley I’ve wanted to do this. You don’t play fair. Where was your bra?” His voice was heavy in her ear.

“My dress was strapless and we were in such a hurry I didn’t…”

Before joining her on the bed, he removed his phone from his pants pocket and turned it off. “There isn’t anything going on in the world that’s more important than what’s going on in here.” He dropped the phone on the table.

His tongue surrounded one nipple, while his other hand kneaded the other. She closed her eyes. His skillful hands teased her. She couldn’t stop grinding her hips against the mattress.

She reached inside his pants. His rod was easy to find. The size and heft of his penis surprised her. His thickness pulsed in her palm.

He wasn’t in a hurry. Time didn’t exist in the dim bedroom. He took as much time with one breast as the other. Her body hummed under his touch. All the reasons for staying away from him evaporated in the desire that held her captive.

He released the buttons on her jeans and helped her out of them. He took his time removing her panties, moving them down her legs one inch at a time while he held eye contact with her. After she was undressed, he removed the rest of his clothes.

Seeing him fully naked was as much a turn on as everything else he'd done to her.

It was foolish to think what she saw blazing in his dark eyes was love. No matter how much she wanted this moment to be a turning point for them, it would never happen. He was a certain man and she was a certain woman. But for now, she was more content than she'd been in years. She wanted to enjoy the moment and not cloud it with reason.

He kissed his way back up her body, starting at her feet, then moving along her calves, each one of them. His treatment of her thighs was the same. She couldn't help squirming. Her thoughts turned to release.

At the meeting of her thighs he paused. He planted a tender kiss at the entrance to her core.

"Are you going to tease me all night?" she asked.

"You're going to let me stay all night? I thought you were going to ask me to leave after we shagged."

"Very funny."

He inserted his tongue into her core. The audible sigh she released matched her pleasure. His skills were unmatched by any of the men before him. All those other times she'd thought she was having great sex, but Richard gave her a whole new definition. There had only been three others, so he didn't have much competition, but she was certain nothing ever felt this good, and sex with anyone else would always be measured by this moment.

She arched her back. He found the center of her pleasure and focused his attention there. She gathered tufts of his hair in each hand. The need to touch some part of him was overwhelming. Just when she was certain she couldn't resist him another moment, he withdrew.

"Perfect timing. I was almost there." She didn't care if he picked up the need in her voice. There was no way she could hide her desire. It was written on every cell of her body.

"It's a gift." He kissed her belly button.

She slid from under him and straddled his lower torso. The junction of her thighs rested on his hard penis. She rocked her hips back and forth to make sure she was as good a tease as he had been. With her head buried in the curve of his neck she sucked on his tender skin. It was his turn to moan. By the sounds coming from him, she was doing everything right. He grabbed a handful of her butt, squeezing it so tight she had to wiggle free.

Within three seconds he was on top of her, again.

She smacked his shoulder. "Condom!"

"Yeah. Right." He leaned off the bed without allowing her to get free. From his wallet, he removed three condoms.

"Put it on me, won't you, love?"

"Why? Are you afraid I'll mount you again and have you clawing the wall?"

"That's exactly it. Now will you please hurry?"

She rolled it into place and spread her legs. He eased into her. The sensation of having him washed over her like a massive wave. For a moment neither of them moved, but she could feel him pulsing inside her.

Their mouths met in a hurried kiss, before he slowed his tongue. She rotated her hips under him. Slowly at first, he matched her gyrations. He eased in and out, every thrust felt like the first one. The pressure mounting in her loins increased. She wanted to go all night, but her body was too sensitive. Every nerve ending fired for satisfaction. When she couldn't delay the ecstasy another moment, she stopped fighting the sensation and was swept away. Dragged in a current of emotion she didn't know existed. Her heart seemed to reach out to him, tying the two of them together in an unbreakable bond. She wanted to fight the passion, but it consumed her like an inferno.

He stiffened a second later, pushing deeper into her. Laying claim to a part of her that was off limits. That was protected from the harsh reality of relationships and love. As they shuddered together she knew she'd gone too far.

Chapter Ten

Renee woke up before the sun poked through the night sky. Next to her in the bed Richard's breathing was even, quiet, peaceful. He was still asleep. She pushed up, careful not to wake him.

With her arms wrapped around her knees, she squeezed her eyes shut. Nothing good could become of getting involved with him. Pretending to be tough enough to have sex, casually brush off any emotions, move on with her life, without being crippled by the impact was impossible. It was a characteristic she didn't possess. She couldn't even delude herself into thinking she didn't care for Richard. Not anymore.

She looked down at his sleeping face and her heart throbbed with tenderness like it didn't know disappointment, despair, or the crushing hurt of being abandoned. Once again, taking the wrong step was going to cost her. She remained in the same position until he stirred.

"What are you doing awake so early?" Richard tugged at her legs, pulling her back down into the bed.

"Just thinking," she said.

"How long have you been doing that?" His voice was heavy with sleep.

"For what was left of the night." She snuggled next to him. Relishing the few remaining moments they had together.

"It was pretty wicked wasn't it?" He kissed her ear. "And so were you."

"You rescued me last night." She ran her index finger down his abs. Comfortable being next to him, but too exhausted to move. He had three condoms, so they'd made love three times. She didn't think it was possible, but each time was better than the last, scored into her memory for future reference.

"If I could move I'd take a heroic bow." He spoke without opening his eyes, like they were lovers with a long history that didn't require more formality. "I was more than happy to get out of there. All the talk about weddings was getting more depressing by the minute."

"Two more days, then we can escape to our regular lives."

He opened his eyes and faced her. "I'm not so sure that's a good thing. I like being here."

"Why?" She held her breath, willing him to say what her heart wanted to hear. Because of her? Was he reluctant to leave her?

He turned on his back and stared at the ceiling for several moments before answering. "Where do I begin?" He paused. "Working for the family company is not as wonderful or glamorous, or glorious as you might think. You don't start with a clean slate. Instead, the family history is imprinted on it and you're expected to live up to it. I see myself as a creative type. The office is stifling."

He didn't want to stay because of her. Disappointment dropped on her chest like a dead weight. She forced past the sadness. Paynes were supposed to be tough.

"Why don't you quit? Based on this weekend alone, you don't need the pay check." She forced her voice to sound calm and even instead of matching the rapid rate of her heart-beat.

"It doesn't work that way." His harsh chuckle revealed more than his words. "Some things are expected."

"What would you do if you could?"

"Take pictures. I'd be a photographer, living my life through a camera lens."

"I've never even seen you with a camera in your hands. I've never even seen you use your camera phone." She sat up straighter.

"It's better not to rock the boat, especially during this visit. Everyone in the family is examining me to see if I'm ready to take life seriously. They're looking even when I don't know it. No drinking, no absurd ideas of being a photographer." He climbed out of bed and reached in the pocket of his jeans. He extracted his cell phone and hit a few buttons. He pointed it at her. "Smile for the camera."

She scurried to cover her breasts, pulling the sheet up to her chin. "I'm not going to pose nude."

He moved around the bed, his in-your-face nakedness added a comical element as he snapped pictures at several angles.

"Stop, Richard. I don't want my picture taken. My makeup is smeared, my hair is a mess, and I'm naked. I don't want nude pictures of me to show up on the Internet. We already know how badly that can turn out."

"You're a natural beauty. The pale lighting is casting a glow on you."

She pulled the sheet over her head. "I'm not coming out until you stop."

The mattress sagged on her side of the bed. "Okay, I'm done. Take a look at these shots. Imagine what I could have done if I had my camera."

She moved the sheet just enough to see him. When she was sure the camera wasn't pointed at her, she crawled to his side and rested her chin on his shoulder.

The first shot showed her nude from the waist up. The idea that he had a half-naked picture of her on his cell made her anxious. They weren't teenagers. This wasn't acceptable. "You have to delete the picture." She tried to grab the phone from him, but he held it out of reach.

"Let's look at all of them." He kissed her on the mouth.

The angst gnawing at her chest vanished. She sat back on her heels, taking him in. How was it possible to like someone who possessed all the qualities that she didn't want when he had one major flaw? Drinking.

Why was he being nice to her? If she asked him to list the qualities he liked in a woman, she was certain it wouldn't include anything she had, and everything she detested. She was in trouble.

He showed her several photos with the sheet at her chin. "Wow. They're pretty good. Even with my hair, they look artsy."

He nodded. "I'll make you a deal. I'll delete the first one, if you let me keep the others."

She sat crossed-legged beside him. "Why would you want pictures of me? On your phone no less?"

He stared at the photo gallery with a vacant stare. Was he thinking about the pictures, or longing for a drink or yearning for another woman? She wanted to be the center of his thoughts, but a worldly man like him was probably only indulging on the available female stock this weekend.

"I really would hate to delete it. I think the first one is best."

"Not open for debate. It's got to go. I want to see your finger move it to the trash. I know this isn't the first time you've been involved in naked pictures and blackmail. And if I see any of those pictures on the Internet, I'll hunt you down and maul you like a lioness who hasn't eaten in weeks. Egypt was devastated when she returned home from the Christmas holiday with the McKinneys. Blackmail doesn't happen to middle-class people from Washington."

"The whole deal was more complicated than you know. Janie has a way of manipulating people to get what she wants, and at the time she wanted to get back at Declan. What did I know?" He continued to look at his phone.

"You should have asked Declan what he wanted. Instead you and Janie bullied Egypt."

"If Egypt really loved Declan she would have fought for him."

"Everything isn't a competition. Love isn't supposed to hurt or require a battle." The conversation stirred up emotions she wanted to forget. "Are you going to delete the pictures? They make me uncomfortable."

After several moments he did as she requested.

"Okay, let me see the phone. I want to make sure you didn't do some sleight of hand gesture," she said.

"Suit yourself. I'm a man of my word. I only kept the one, the picture with the sheet over your face." He held the phone out to her and she checked several apps. When she was confident with her search, she jumped off the bed and snapped several pictures of him. Instead of covering up, he posed fully nude for her.

"Oh, it's easy for you. The pictures are on your phone. You have nothing to worry about."

"No, that's not the only reason. The human form is beautiful. I'm not some naughty boy who would have texted your pictures to my friends."

"Then you won't mind if I text this picture to me." She hit the send button, half expecting him to object. But he didn't move.

"I tricked you, didn't I? You thought I was going to go bananas, but it doesn't bother me. My only request is that you don't post it on Facebook or Instagram."

She neared the bed. "Ah, come on. I want to show my sisters how I spent my time in Glen Cove."

"Then come back to bed and let's give you something more to share." He held out his hand to her.

It was becoming a theme for them. He kept inviting her to do things she'd have sworn she'd never do.

"Any minute now everyone in the house will be awake. It's going to be a day of boys going one way and girls going another, so you better come get what I've got for you." He drew closer.

"Without any more condoms, we aren't having any more fun." She kissed his mouth.

"I'll pull out. You have my word."

She held his chin in her palm. The scruff on his face tickled. "Do I look that naïve? I'll admit you've had me do several things I wouldn't normally do, but I'm not falling for the biggest lie ever told." She climbed across him, making sure her breast brushed his lips as she got off the bed. She gathered his clothes and handed them to him. "I'll see you at breakfast."

He nodded and waved her closer to the bed.

"How do you do it, Renee?" he asked while holding her hand.

"What?"

"Whenever you're in public you're all smiles, like you're having a ball here. But I heard you in the powder room last night. And even when we were alone at the bowling alley, I could tell something was troubling you."

She tilted her head, so sure she was hiding her baggage. He was her issue. He was the thing that made her sad this weekend. Being this close to something she couldn't have was torture. "It's Egypt's weekend. For her I put on my game face. Besides, everyone is snapping pictures all over the place. No one wants to look back at their wedding pictures and see a sour puss maid-of-honor."

"You are remarkable. Always looking out for somebody else." He ran his hand along her jaw.

"It's not as hard as you think."

He got out of bed behind her. For several seconds, he held her eyes. His lips were pursed, as if he was going to say something else. But he didn't. His erection faded, but he still looked magnificent. To erase the unspoken tension between them, she extended her arm again, hoping his pants would distract his gaze. He stepped into his pants and shirt, without the briefs or the socks.

"I'll get more condoms. For tonight." He wrapped his arms around her and held her tight.

"We'll see." She was afraid to meet his eyes. The line she didn't want to cross had been breached. What started out as casual sex last night was feeling more meaningful with the morning sun shining on it. And if she was the only one sharing the connection, she didn't want to see it in his eyes.

He kissed her again. His fingers lingered on her neck, leaving a trail of heat behind. She was tempted to draw him back into bed, without the protection of the condoms, but hushed voices in the hall snapped her back into reality.

"Don't let anyone see you leaving."

"Why? We're adults. You're not ashamed of me are you?" He pressed his back against the door.

"No," she said without looking at his face. She grabbed his boxers and socks from his hand. "Leave this stuff here. Just in case."

"Are you giving me an invitation to return? It was quite a fantastic shag, wasn't it?" He put his hand on the doorknob. "And just in case I didn't say it earlier, you have a body that should grace the centerfold of Playboy. But to really appreciate it, you'd have to be fully nude and I hear they don't do full nudity any longer. As soon as their sales drop, they'll go back to what made them money, though."

"You might not know this, but I used to have a crush on you. Of course that was before you almost jacked up Egypt's relationship with Declan." The need to keep her feeling for him a secret wasn't important any more. The shield between them had come down.

He stepped toward her and cuddled her closer. "I didn't know. You were always so tough. I didn't think you liked anyone. But since we're being honest, I had a thing for you, too."

"You don't have to say you like me just because I said it."

He winked, opened the door and disappeared.

"Oh, we're going to finish that conversation." She placed her hands on her hips.

Chapter Eleven

Renee twirled across the room and fell back on the tousled bed. She wrapped the sheet around her and tried to silence the sledgehammer slamming in her heart. Nothing about the weekend was real or concrete or forever, but for the next few minutes she allowed herself to indulge in every memory imprinted on her brain. His smell, his taste, his touch loitered in the emptiness he'd left behind and she soaked it up before it dissipated.

She showered and dressed. Being the last one to enter the dining room for breakfast would garner some stares. She was certain everyone would be able to tell she was trying to hide something. The stain of the hot night she'd shared with Richard had to be written where everyone could see it. She examined her neck in the mirror for passion marks before leaving the bedroom.

At the top of the stairs, Richard was leaning against the wall, scrolling through his cell phone.

"What are you doing here?" Her tone was as light as her footsteps. She was happy and wanted to wallow in it.

"Waiting on you." He held out a hand. "Shall we." He led her down the steps.

Giddy because he'd waited for her. If she closed her eyes tight she could almost make herself believe he was feeling just a bit of what she was feeling. He was everything she'd dreamed he'd be, only better. If she could subtract the drinking he'd be downright delicious.

The dining room was almost full. There weren't two seats together. More people streamed into the house every day. Egypt's parents were seated at one end of the room, engaged in a conversation with Declan's parents. Wedding details, no doubt.

No one seemed to notice as she and Richard took seats across the table from each other. Her body was a torrent of emotion, as if one side was fighting the other, a battle of common sense over lust, love, and libido.

There was no way her friends didn't notice what was going on with her. She felt too different for anyone to think she was the same.

She took a seat at the table, and filled her plate with scrambled eggs and Canadian bacon with no intention of eating any of it. There wasn't any room in her stomach for anything more until she sorted out her life.

Egypt stood up and clicked her spoon against the empty glass of juice. "We have a coach that's going to pick us up in a few minutes. We're going to a cottage to be pampered before the nuptials tonight."

Yani stood. "I'm in need of some special treatment." She pumped her fist in the air. "I feel like this baby is already taking over my body."

If she had any idea Maxi was trying to make nice with her husband she would probably be glued to his side all day.

Renee snuck a glance at Richard. He looked up and caught her eye. She expected him to direct his attention away. Pretend nothing between the two of them had changed, the way she was trying. Instead, he held her gaze long enough for anyone paying attention to see the flicker of something there. What did he see when he looked at her? Did he see her shortcomings, that she was damaged? She no longer saw him as the alcoholic or the rude Brit. The safety net that was supposed to protect her had evaporated along with all inhibitions in the heated sheets last night. She needed to refocus. There was too much at stake to pretend otherwise.

She jumped up from the table. "I'm with you, Yani. I'm ready. Let me get my coat. I'll be back in less than a minute."

By the time the six of them huddled in the coach, Renee was able to act normal, even though guilt riddled her with doubt. No one could see how her skin still tingled from his touch, and she relaxed.

It didn't take long to reach the cottage. From outside, the stone façade building could have passed as a mid-priced home, but inside the elegance was unmistakable. The spa was right in line with everything else attached to the wedding festivities.

As soon as they reached the reception desk, an overzealous attendant descended on them. "Egypt Carrington party?"

"Yes, we have appointments for massages, manicures, pedicures, and a late buffet lunch." Egypt pulled a sheet of paper from her purse and checked it. "There are six of us."

The attendant scanned her clipboard. "There are two more women in the waiting room who said they will be joining your party."

Egypt hunched her shoulders. "No, that can't be right. There are only five girls in the wedding party and we're all here." She glanced at the clipboard. With her index finger she pointed at the names. "Yani, Phoebe, Geeta, Cat, and Renee. We're all here. There must be some mistake."

"The young lady arrived a few minutes ago. She said she is your sister-in-law, Maxi McKinney, and her friend's name is Janie Atwood. She said you wouldn't mind." The attendant's eyes grew large.

Egypt took a noticeable breath, her face felt hot. She loosened the scarf around her neck. She needed air.

"You can follow the runner to the lounge where they're waiting." The attendant said, before hurrying behind a nearby door.

Egypt turned to face her wedding party. "I don't believe this. Is this what being married to Declan is going to be like, always having to suck up my feelings?"

"Who is Janie? What's the big deal?" Geeta stepped forward and placed her hand on Egypt's shoulder.

"She's the one who was in cahoots with Richard. She used to date Declan, or she wanted to date him. And she's the one who dug up the nude picture of Egypt," Renee answered for the bride-to-be because she looked like her tongue was on lock-down.

"Well, just because she's here doesn't mean she has to ruin our day." Phoebe pushed forward to stand next to Egypt. "How about this? Let's split up into two groups. Renee and I will partner with the two interlopers. And the three of you can be in the other group. You won't have to lay eyes on Janie all day. We'll see to it." She slapped high five with Renee.

Egypt didn't move.

"We got you, Egypt. Janie won't cause you any trouble. Come on Phoebe." Renee beckoned her friend towards the waiting area. "We'll do pedicures first and make sure she stays out of your way." She kissed Egypt on the cheek. One day someone was going to come to her rescue, so she was racking up a boatload of brownie points.

Renee tried to sound more confident than she actually was. She'd never met Janie, but from the stories Egypt shared, Janie had very little integrity and was a master in cutthroat antics.

"I know Janie's a family friend, but for her to show up at this bridal event takes brass balls." Phoebe talked through clenched teeth. The veins in her neck bulged. Out of the whole crew, she had the reputation for being the toughest. And all her skills might be needed to handle Janie.

"Calm down, Phoebe. We might have a very long day dealing with Janie. Maxi isn't going to be an issue. She's just young and rambunctious. According to Egypt, she's not even sure the whole family knows what happened back in Europe."

"Why do you think Janie is here?"

"Maybe this is her last attempt to break up Declan and Egypt." The words left a rotting taste on her tongue. "Egypt deserves to be happy. She deserves the fairy tale wedding and it's our job to make sure she gets it." Renee stood up straighter, ready to do battle.

They entered the small lounge. Maxi was seated next to a beautiful blonde with legs as long as lampposts. She was prettier than Renee had imagined. With beauty like that, she had to be used to getting her way.

"I hope you guys don't mind but we decided to join you." Maxi was like a puppy, bumbling over her big paws. Insulated by privilege, she thought everyone was good and only happiness existed in her world. "Janie called me this morning and I invited her along. Where's everyone else?" She looked over Renee's shoulder.

"The group was too large, so we had to split into two. We're going to do pedicures first." Phoebe was in official mode. Her voice was clipped and professional.

"That sounds lovely." Janie stood, towering over everyone except Phoebe by several inches. She reeked of money, with her thousand-dollar over-the-knee Chloe boots and cashmere leggings. "I do hope Egypt doesn't mind me coming along. I really do need a massage after that long flight. I feel like I'm all in knots." She wiggled her shoulders.

"It's not a problem. Egypt knows you're not a threat. Will the rest of your family be attending the wedding tomorrow?" Renee asked.

"Of course I'm not a threat to Egypt and Declan. That's water under the bridge. My parents wouldn't miss the wedding. They're quite fond of Declan." She clapped her manicured hands together. "Their flight gets in later this morning."

Renee would have sworn Janie tilted her nose just a millimeter higher while talking to her.

"Ladies, the technicians are ready for you. I'll show you to the dressing room where you can change into your warm robes."

"This is going to be fun. Let's go." Maxi took off ahead of them, followed by Janie.

Renee shook her head. This weekend was not shaping up the way she thought. Not at all.

They managed to change and make their way to the pedicure recliners without exchanging rude comments or evil glances. If the balance of the afternoon ticked by as smoothly, then they wouldn't have any trouble.

"Janie, I have to admit it takes some guts to show up at your ex's wedding. If it were me, I think I'd rather spend the day in the arms of a new love instead of witnessing the nuptials of the one who got away." Phoebe reclined in her chair. Her comment left a crackle in the air that could be heard over the whirlpools.

"Declan and I were never serious. We've been friends since grade school." She twirled one of her long blond tresses around her index finger. "Actually I was hoping to spend a little more time with Richard. I have a yummy secret to share with him."

Janie's giddy announcement made Renee's lungs seize up, making it hard to breathe. Cold tentacles of dread pressed against her body, creeping across her skin like death coming to claim her dreams.

Dreams she couldn't have.

Dreams were for normal people.

She wasn't one of those girls with frilly, fantastic memories. She hadn't been normal since she uncovered her parents' secret.

Her father's drinking was no surprise.

But his abuse was.

She wrapped her arms around her waist to stop her body from shaking. An explosion of emotions flamed in her head like fireworks. She forced her body to stay erect, to function like normal, because this was the kind of insanity she was used to.

The monster had crawled from under the bed, just as she expected it would. It had been lurking, waiting for her to think life could be ordinary. Now the monster danced on her heart, laughed at her stupidity. How could she think that a relationship with Richard was plausible? It was the most ridiculous thought she'd ever had.

"I love secrets. What is it?" Maxi sat forward in her chair like an excited child. Her eyes dazzled with anticipation. But she wasn't the only one who wanted to hear Janie's news.

"Oh, no. I must talk to him first." Janie's smug smile heightened the curiosity. "I tried to call him last night when I arrived, but he didn't pick up."

The clog in Renee's throat grew. The vision of Richard turning off his phone the night before was as clear as if he'd just done it a moment ago. The slick feel of her tongue against the roof of her mouth made her cough.

"How long have you and Richard been seeing each other?" Renee squeezed the words out.

"Well we're not exactly seeing each other. We've spent a few nights together. I think we can turn it into something more." Sweetness dripped from Janie's voice like maple syrup.

"Over lunch we'll have to make sure to celebrate you and Richard. We're all wishing you the best." Phoebe had no idea how deep her words cut.

No one did.

What sounded innocent and uplifting knocked the wind out of Renee. The balance of the day she willed her way through the activities that were supposed to relax the wedding party. Instead, each one wound her tighter.

There was nobody to blame for her discomfort. It would have been wonderful to say everything was Janie's fault. She wasn't invited to their party. She wasn't welcome in their group. She wasn't supposed to impact their lives. And as the reminders crisscrossed through Renee's head, she grew angry with herself.

She only had two tasks to accomplish this weekend. To make sure Egypt was happy, and to keep Richard away from alcohol. To think it was an opportunity for anything more had been a mistake. To think she wanted to be with Richard had also been a mistake. He had as much baggage as she did and his was as toxic as hers.

It was impossible to enjoy lunch. Conversation buzzed around her and her body absorbed it all like a sponge. Taking in the tidbits about weddings, and the pieces of family gossip and the best places to honeymoon, left her body rigid. She couldn't process all the chatter. Making it through the wedding only hours away was going to challenge her more than anything else. How was she supposed to approach Richard? The idea of facing him was too painful to anticipate.

Chapter Twelve

The wedding party and Maxi boarded the coach to return to the house. Renee's major wound was invisible to the naked eye, but she felt the scar across her heart each time she took a breath.

"Renee, you've been quiet. Did you enjoy the spa?" Egypt sat on the front row and had to turn to see the others.

"I'm fine. It was a lot of fun." Renee pumped her voice full of enthusiasm.

"Thank you and Phoebe for handling this little situation for me," Egypt said.

"What? Did something happen?" Maxi was seated in the last row of the coach, alone.

"Maxi, I want to talk to you about what it means to be a sister. Not a relative, sister, but a soul sister." Egypt met the eyes of her friends. "As your sister-in-law, I need to know you've got my back. That I can depend on you." Egypt's voice shook with emotion.

"Of course. You can count on me. We McKinneys are big on family." Maxi's response rang hollow with Renee. Maxi didn't know how to live up to her words and Renee could tell the difference. The

Payne family could quote the same kind of empty promises. Her father's favorite was *I love my girls*. Too bad he didn't love them enough to give them the security they'd needed while growing up.

"In less than four hours I'll be family. I hope if you have to make a choice going forward, you'll pick me over Janie." Egypt's voice was sharp.

"I shouldn't have invited her to the spa, huh?" Maxi's immaturity was evident in the innocence of her eyes.

"It was *my* event. I'm the one who made the decision on who was invited. You didn't have the right to tell Janie or to invite her." Egypt turned to face the windshield.

"I'm sorry," she paused. "I get it." The overwhelming puppy excitement was gone.

"Wow," Renee spoke to Egypt low so Maxi couldn't hear. "When did you get so tough?"

"If you're not tough, this family will crush you under their designer boots. I learned that the hard way."

Renee settled back in her seat. Warning bells clanged in her head, even louder than they had before she left home. Janie's appearance made the ringing more intense. Putting her emotions back in check wouldn't be easy now. Until the spa visit, the weekend she'd been dreading had turned into a fairy tale. Like most fairy tales, there was evil lurking close by.

"What did the guys do today?" Geeta asked.

"They probably opened a strip club early and had a private party around a pole." Phoebe chuckled, but there was a hint of curiosity in her reply. "Do you know, Maxi?"

"I'm a quick learner. I'm not saying anything." Maxi's reply made them all laugh.

"Okay, okay." Egypt clapped her hands to get their attention. "We've had our nails done, our toes done, we've had massages and facials. When we get back to the house, it will be show time." She paused for a long moment. "I'm getting married this evening. I'm going to marry…" Tears appeared in her eyes and her bottom lip trembled.

Renee reached over the seat and placed her hand on Egypt's shoulder. "I was wondering when you were going to get emotional. We're all here. It's going to be great."

"Yes, Egypt. It's obvious Declan loves you as much as you love him. You two make each other happy," said Cat.

"I know. I know. It's just…for a long time I didn't think I was ever going to find someone to make me feel like this. I kept meeting a bunch of duds."

"We've all kissed our share of frogs," said Yani.

"Some of us are still kissing frogs," said Renee. "I guess not everyone is destined to marry and have children. The word spinster was added to the dictionary just for me."

A wave of 'ahs' filled the coach. She wasn't looking for sympathy, only adjusting to reality. The sooner she owned it, the less painful it was going to be.

"Hey, don't feel sorry for me, guys. I'm going to be just fine. I can come visit you guys and play with your children, hang out and have fun with you, and then when it's time to do the domestic stuff, I can go back to my place and put my feet up. I won't have to learn the word compromise. Life is good." Renee was so convincing she almost believed it, too.

The coach pulled into the drive and most of the cars were still gone. Wherever the guys went, it looks like they haven't returned yet," Geeta said.

"They'll be back. I'm not worried." Egypt said and there was conviction in her voice. She must have been confident in Declan's love for her.

The coach stopped in front of the house and they all climbed out. Maxi was the first to go inside. No doubt happy to get away just in case Egypt had another admonishment to pass along.

"Will you guys please get dressed in my room? That way my mother won't force her way in and give me advice I don't need. And I'm hoping you guys will keep me grounded, keep me from flying away…you know."

They gathered around Egypt, giving her a hug. A small wave of relief flooded through Renee. She had the excuse she needed to hide from Richard, just in case he decided to stop by her room. There was a tiny spot in her belly that wanted him to knock on her door and be disappointed she wasn't there. The chance of him coming to her now that Janie was here was nil, but she held on to the thought.

"I think that's a wonderful idea. I should have thought of it." Renee smacked her forehead. "I'll get my things."

"Give us a couple of minutes and we'll be there." Yani yelled over her shoulder, then ran ahead of Renee into the house.

Renee charged up the stairs, taking them two at a time. By the time she reached her room she was winded. She took a deep breath before opening the bedroom door. The memories of the night before were still fresh. Maybe they always would be.

The room wasn't the way she'd left it. The bed was made. Richard's socks and boxers were nowhere in sight and the bathroom had fresh white linens. If only it was so easy to swipe away everything else.

She gathered her make-up kit and shoved it into the bag with her wedding gear. With her gown over her arm she maneuvered her things out the door. Getting out of the room was the only thing that mattered.

She knocked on Egypt's door. She heard voices coming from inside the room.

Egypt opened the door. "Mom, Renee is here. The other girls will be here in a minute and we'll need to get dressed. I'll see you and dad just before coming downstairs."

"Okay, okay. I'm going. I just wanted to see my baby before she becomes a Mrs." Mrs. Carrington picked up her handbag. "Take care of my baby, Renee." She placed a kiss on Renee's cheek.

Renee closed the door. "You kicked your mother out?"

"She's still giving me a hard time for having the wedding here and not in some big church in D.C. that we never even attended, so she could put on a show for people who I don't even know." She flopped on the bed and crossed her arms. "I'm not as interested in the wedding as I am in the marriage. I can't wait to spend my life with Declan. For me this weekend has been all about our marriage, not the wedding."

Renee sat beside her. "I don't think I've ever seen you this happy. And no one deserves it more than you."

"I've never been this happy—" A soft knock on the door cut her off. Renee jumped up and opened it for Cat, Yani, Geeta, and Phoebe.

"Okay, now let's dish the dirt on what Janie had to say," Phoebe said before the door was even closed.

Egypt glanced at Renee, an eyebrow raised.

"Don't look at me. She didn't tell us what the big secret was. Only that it involved Richard, so don't worry," Renee said.

"Maybe he asked her to marry him." Cat flopped in a nearby chair.

"Maybe the two of them are plotting some more havoc for some unsuspecting soul," Geeta chimed in.

Renee winced. Geeta was half right. The only difference was Renee wasn't unsuspecting. She knew better than to let her guard down with Richard, yet she had.

"We have four hours to get ready. That's plenty of time to share a glass of wine before we start to dress." Egypt picked up the phone and began to dial. "I'll ask someone to bring us a bottle and several glasses. We need to celebrate."

Chapter Thirteen

The huge living room had been transformed into a Valentine wonderland for the wedding ceremony. The chandeliers were dimmed, and threaded with pink and emerald bows. Each one had a puffed pink heart dangling from its center. Evergreens and chrysanthemums lined the room.

Their fragrant smell reminded Renee of the Christmas she'd spent with her family just months ago. At least there had been no major drama. Her father drank plain eggnog without complaint and no one asked her about her love life.

Standing just inches away from Richard while Egypt and Declan said their vows was more difficult than Renee anticipated. Each time she looked up, she caught him staring. Her stomach refused to settle down. It couldn't be the two bottles of wine they drank while dressing because she only pretended to take a sip. No one seemed to notice she was only faking her smiles.

She glanced up from her bouquet and caught his eyes. This time instead of refocusing on something else, she held his gaze. How could one man be charming, and tender, while being a drinker and a womanizer? He was everything she wanted and everything she didn't. Tears stung at her eyes. She bit them back and turned her head.

The hum of the vows continued. Zeroing in on the words was the only way to push thoughts of Richard away. Her heart pressed against her chest. Within minutes she was going to have to take Richard's arm and walk between the rows of chairs leading to the ballroom.

She took a deep breath. The hard part of the weekend was almost over. She'd take his arm and continue to pretend everything was just fine, because in time it would be. Time had a way of dulling the past. She was certain of that.

The priest pronounced Declan and Egypt, husband and wife. The newlyweds kissed so long everyone began to applaud them. They ended their kiss on their own time, then linked arms and headed out of the room.

Richard held out his arm for her. Without hesitating, she took it and marched out behind Declan and Egypt. She caught a glimpse of Janie as they exited the room. Janie's eyes blazed at Richard. He didn't acknowledge her.

"Where have you been? I've been looking for you all evening." he whispered in her ear.

"I've been helping Egypt." She smiled for the flashing cameras.

"All day?"

"That's why we're here, isn't it?" she said through her frozen smile.

They entered the reception hall and lined up the way they were instructed for the receiving line.

"Can I talk to you?"

"Maybe later, Richard. After this we've got a lot to do…the dance, the dinner, the…"

"Okay, later tonight."

She nodded. And shook hands with the first person through the line. No matter what happened she was going to be mature. She'd consented to everything that happened. And most of it was pretty amazing. The weekend she'd been dreading, was more fun than she'd ever imagined. For that she couldn't be sorry or unhappy. Richard had never been available to her, but it had been fun playing make believe for a while.

"Richard, I've been trying to get in touch with you." Janie kissed him on the mouth and embraced him in more than a friendly hug. "I've been ringing your mobile since I got into town." She placed the palm of her hand flat against his chest. The intimate gesture left Renee dazed. Her knees almost buckled.

"Hello, Janie. I cut my phone off last night and forgot to turn it back on." He looked at Renee before turning back to Janie. "Can we talk later? I don't want to hold up the line."

"Sure. We've got all night. I have something I need to share with you." Janie kissed him again, this time on the cheek.

"Renee, I'd like for you to meet my parents." Richard gestured to the next couple in line. The resemblance between Richard and the man shaking his hand was striking. They both were over six feet tall, and even though Richard's father's hair was more white than black, the rich texture was the same. So were their features. Richard was a younger version of his handsome, debonair father.

"Well, hello Renee. Aren't you a beautiful woman? You remind me of brown sugar." He lifted her hand to his lips and kissed it.

"Oh, Dick, this young lady isn't the least bit impressed by you. Keep the line moving." Richard's mother nudged him. "Please excuse him, honey. No matter how old he gets, he still thinks women swoon over him. I keep hoping he'll outgrow his roving eyes, but I've learned to live with it." There was humor in her voice, but none in her eyes.

"It's nice to meet you." Renee shook his mother's hand. No wonder Richard's life was beset with problems, his apple hadn't fallen far enough away from the family tree.

After they had progressed further down the receiving line, Richard leaned to her ear. "Ignore my parents, most people do."

"You take after your father, don't you?" She couldn't help but be a bit sarcastic. Janie's appearance had shed a new light on Richard. One she didn't want to examine too closely.

"I'm nothing at all like my father." His tone was harsh. He accepted the next guest's hand, turning his back to her.

It didn't take long for the line to end. It was a small wedding. The elegant dinner that followed was handled with the precision of a military drill. Renee mustered all her charm to be the best maid-of-honor in McKinney-Carrington history. By the time the dancing and drinking started, her cheeks ached from all the smiling.

"I think the hardest part of the day is over." Cat came up behind Renee and handed her a slice of cake.

"Yep. Look at Egypt. I don't think I've ever seen her happier." Renee pointed across the room. Declan and Egypt chatted with Egypt's parents. He had his arm around her waist. The two of them had been inseparable all evening.

"How are you holding up?" Phoebe joined their group. She'd taken off her shoes and held them on her fingers.

Renee breathed out of her mouth. "I'm good. I think my work here is done."

"It looks like Janie finally got her chance to talk to Richard." Phoebe pointed across the room.

Renee followed her glance. Richard had Janie penned in the far corner of the ballroom. From where she stood, the two of them looked like every other cozy couple attending the wedding. Renee stood ramrod straight, ignoring the sudden urge to double over. The pain of seeing them together cut her heart in two.

Watching Richard with someone else made her woozy. Even though he was off limits, the possibility of him had been fun to experience. But the winter wonderland was coming to an end. It was time to go home, back to reality.

Renee watched Janie stroke Richard's face. Their intimacy was more than she wanted to see.

"Egypt and Declan are getting ready to leave. We better get over to her," Renee forced the words out pass the lump in her throat. The smile she'd worn all night was still in place. It would take days for her face to return to normal.

"Renee, you're the only one of us who is eligible to catch the bouquet. Don't you want to get up there?" Yani asked and nudged her forward at the same time.

She looked up to catch a glimpse of Richard leading Janie onto the balcony. The temperature outside was below freezing, which meant their need for privacy must have been more important than warmth.

"I better leave that to someone who's on the threshold of love. Without any prospects on the horizon, I just might become the crazy aunt living in the basement." She hoped she sounded more jovial than bitter, because ice was forming around her heart, sealing it off from pain.

Standing in the back of the excited crowd with her friends eased the angst in her chest. She was glad she had them. Seeing Richard with Janie hurt more than it should, but she was going to be okay. Getting back on familiar territory where the comparison of her life against others wasn't as stark would be a relief.

"Declan and I will be gone for a month. As soon as I get back let's plan to get together." Egypt spoke to the six of them, including them in her gaze. "I'm sure we've got lots of stories to share about this weekend."

"You bet we do." Yani nodded. "I'll plan it."

Renee reached for Egypt's hand. "Be happy, girl."

"If I was any happier I think I'd be sickening. You guys have made this weekend the best." She kissed each of them before Declan signaled it was time for them to go.

Without the newlyweds there, there was no one for the crowd to gather around. The room began to empty. Renee surveyed the room one last time for Richard. Neither he nor Janie were anywhere in sight.

She folded her lips and nodded. She'd been the appetizer. Now with Janie here, he had his entrée.

Back in the quiet of her suite, Renee kicked off her satin shoes and flopped on the bed. She exhaled long and slow through her mouth. Egypt was pleased with how everything turned out, so the insurmountable had been accomplished.

Coming out of the pretty emerald gown wasn't the culmination to the evening she'd anticipated. A frosty finger enclosed her heart at the thought of riding back to D.C. with him in the morning.

Would she be designated to the back seat to make room for Janie in the front?

Would she be expected to pretend nothing of importance happened between her and Richard?

Would she be able to bury her feelings for him?

Chapter Fourteen

Renee crawled into bed. With her bags packed and sitting by the door, the morning wouldn't come fast enough. The only thing that buoyed her was getting back to the routine she knew, the one she controlled.

She reached for her phone, half hoping Richard had called or texted while she was in the shower. Nothing. It was almost 2:00 AM. She pressed the photo gallery icon on her phone. The picture of Richard popped up. She scanned his silhouette, hoping to find an imperfection. There weren't any visible, but the ones no one could see were far worse. He should have worn a sign around his neck warning her he could be hazardous to her health.

She lay very still and listened for a noise from his room. The house was so quiet it was eerie. She turned off the light. In the dark room shadows from the trees played against the ceiling.

A rap on the door startled her. She jumped out of bed to answer it. Her heartbeat increased with each step. She hoped it was Richard. The only person she didn't need to see.

She opened the door just enough to peek out. Richard stood in the hall, still dressed in his tux, even though his bowtie dangled from its collar.

"What are you doing here?"

"Please let me in. I don't want anyone to see me out here." He glanced down the hall towards the stairs.

She opened the door wider to allow him in.

"Why have you been ignoring me all day? What's going on? I thought…I—"

"Janie happened, Richard." She pressed her hand to her throat. The short nightgown exposed her breast and her butt.

He dropped his head. "You know?"

She sat on the bed and used the sheet to cover her legs. "I know she's here for you. I know she had something yummy to tell you. Her words not mine."

He released a loud breath. With his back to her, he strolled to the balcony and rested his arm against the door. For several moments neither of them spoke. His posture was different.

"I get it, Richard. You and Janie have a thing. Don't worry about me. I'm not the kind of girl who expected anything from you. I appreciate you coming here to tell me, but you really didn't need to." She wanted to sound worldly and sophisticated, as if this kind of turmoil was normal and she wasn't impacted in the least. Her voice faltered at the end.

"She says she's pregnant. She says I'm the father," his words rushed out.

The news was like another punch to her stomach, crushing her under a tidal wave of I-told-you-so. The unbearable weight of his news choked off her breath, daring her to cry or yell or go all girly with emotion.

She blinked a number of times. "I guess I should say congratulations." Instead of looking at him, she stared at her hands in her lap. If she looked at him she was certain she was going to cry.

"Like hell. I always use a condom. We only shagged twice and it happened months ago."

"I guess you're one of those lucky men. One of the two percent who has super human sperm that can penetrate latex. I knew you were special." She snapped her fingers to punctuate her flippant tone.

He turned away from the balcony door to face her. "I really like you, Renee. I know it sounds crazy, but I…I…think we made a connection here. You know Janie can't be trusted. I'll demand a paternity test."

"We had fun, Richard. But we're fooling ourselves if we think we could have anything. I'm just a regular girl, from a messed up family, with a straight nine-to-five job. We have nothing in common." Her voice almost faltered.

"That doesn't matter to me." He sat beside her on the bed. "I've been happier this weekend than I have in the last five years combined. If Janie is pregnant it doesn't mean we become a couple. I don't want to be with her."

"What about the baby?"

"I don't know." He tousled his curls. "My head is killing me. I can't work out the details, but I will. I promise."

She wanted to be angry with him. Mad enough to erase his imprint off her soul. But the look he gave her left her too weak to resist him. This had to be what love felt like, because it was new for her.

He pulled her closer, lifted her chin with his index finger. "Tell me you understand or that you'll at least try?"

"I'm trying. But I don't know, Richard. A baby is a big deal."

He pressed his mouth to hers, pushing his tongue deep into her mouth. Her insides turned over. But she drew away from him and jumped up.

Alarm bells banged against her brain. The deafening sound was loud, overriding the tenderness swelling in her heart. She could love him, but she couldn't be stupid. Not anymore. "You've been drinking?"

He stood too. "I had a glass of champagne." He extended his hands to her, palm sides up.

She ran all ten of her fingers through her hair, pulling at the roots. "No. No. No. You can't. You're an alcoholic." She spun around. Even if she could deal with a baby, she couldn't deal with him drinking. An inebriated Richard was just too scary. More than a baby, it frightened her enough to clear the clutter chugging through her head.

"It was just one glass. A toast. I'm not drunk." He reached for her.

"No. Don't touch me. After what I went through with my father, I thought you'd understand how I felt about men who drink. I can…I won't—not with a man who has a drinking problem. You better go." She pointed to the door. "When you were with me, you were fine. The moment I wasn't hovering over you like some giant pain-in-the-ass, you're drinking. I can't co-sign this. I won't." She marched to the door and yanked it open. "I think you'd better go. Go to your room. Go to Janie. Go anywhere you want, just get away from me. Maybe the two of you are meant for each other. You'll figure it out."

"But, Renee—"

She put up her hand to stop him. "No, Richard, there is no but." She closed the door behind him. "I'll never forget this Valentine's Day."

Chapter Fifteen

Renee was still seated on the edge of the bed when the sun lit up the sky. Her eyes were dry. There had been no tears. She couldn't cry for what might have been. At least she hadn't made a total fool of herself. But she'd come closer than was comfortable.

If she had a second chance, there were lots of things she'd do different. She wouldn't have allowed him in her room, she wouldn't have had sex with him, she wouldn't allow her feelings to play fast and loose with thoughts of him. But at least she'd lived her fantasy. For two full days she had Richard right where she wanted him. She had him in her bedroom at home. She had him in her suite at Glen Cove. And she had him. All of him. The memories danced through her head like fairytales. Ones she'd cherish for a long time.

She showered and dressed in minutes. The need to get home was more pressing. The everyday sameness of work and the familiarity of her routine would ease the sense of abandonment. At least the drive home would be faster than the one to reach Glen Cove. There was no snow to impede their progress.

That is, of course, unless Janie occupied the front seat. But Janie and Richard deserved each other.

There was a knock on her door. If Richard had come back, it had better be to say it was time to get on the road. She didn't want breakfast. She didn't want to talk. She didn't want another explanation.

"Okay, I'm coming." She opened the door to find Maxi. "I wasn't expecting you."

"Richard asked if I'd give you a ride back to D.C. He left early this morning. I'm going down to breakfast and should be ready in about an hour. Is that okay with you?"

Renee looked over Maxi's shoulder as if she expected Richard to be standing there to confirm what she'd just said.

"Is that okay?" Maxi asked again.

"Did…did Richard say why he was leaving early?"

"No. He muttered something about Janie and then asked if I'd take you back when I leave. I have a cute little apartment on North Capital Street. Maybe you'll get a chance to stop in and see it."

"I'll be ready in an hour." Renee closed the door. A feeling of numbness washed over her. She was doing the right thing for the right reasons, but it didn't feel too good. Richard and Janie were probably halfway to Blissville. Her heart twisted. A different kind of loneliness gripped her. Richard wouldn't be easily forgotten.

She called the number beside the phone and requested her bags be placed in Maxi's trunk, then she made her way to the dining room.

Half expecting to see Richard seated at the table, she scanned the room.

Geeta stood up. "I was hoping to catch you this morning. Everyone else left. Brooks and I will be leaving in a few minutes to catch our flight back to Houston." She embraced Renee. "It was a nice wedding, wasn't it?"

"I don't think I've been to a more charming one." Renee cleared her throat. "I'm sure your wedding was awesome, you know what I mean."

"Don't worry. Now you know why Brooks and I decided to run off. I didn't want to deal with all the hoopla," said Geeta.

"I'm with you. If I'm lucky enough to find Mr. Right, I'm going to sneak off and marry him and live happily ever after. I'm not going to test the wedding gods into making me the princess for a day. I'll be thankful I finally found my man."

"Amen to that." They laughed together.

Renee and Geeta finished breakfast just as Maxi waved her hand, signaling she was ready to leave. Renee kissed her friend, and made her way to the door. Leaving Glen Cove was like tearing a bandage off a wound. She needed to, but she didn't want to. Not yet. Not without seeing Richard once more. She bit down on her lip and stepped outside into the cold winter air.

"I asked Duke to bring the car to the front door and warm it up for us. I hate getting into a cold car, don't you?" Maxi climbed behind the driver's seat.

"I don't have a Duke to preheat my car, so no, I don't mind. I did the next best thing. I bought a car with heated seats." Renee strapped on her seatbelt.

"You're very funny."

Renee nodded. It was going to be a long ride and not nearly as comfortable as the roomy seats in Richard's car. Maxi drove a low to the ground sports car. Every bump in the road was exaggerated.

"Richard was in a hurry to get away. He said he didn't think you'd mind getting a lift from me."

"This is fine. I'm just glad to be going home. Glen Cove is nice, but I wouldn't want to live there." Renee looked out the passenger side window. Snow still covered the ground and clung to some of the trees, but the roads were clear. This was a beautiful place, but she wouldn't miss it.

"Richard and I are a lot alike. I'm adopted and he feels like an outsider, so we spend a lot of time talking about our status in the family. We both feel the need to fit in with a family who doesn't make it easy. They don't do it on purpose. I don't think they know how difficult it is. I stand out like a sore thumb, with my brown skin and my thick wooly hair."

"Yeah, I get it. I felt out of place this weekend, too. Your family is very nice. But I'm just not used to all the stuff. The servants. The big house. Plenty of everything." For a moment they were quiet. Asking questions about Richard probably wasn't fair to Maxi, but in the car, propriety didn't seem as important. "Why doesn't Richard feel comfortable in his own family?"

"It's all about his father. He's a bit of a fuck-up. Years ago, even before Richard was born, he embezzled money from the company, so his father fired him. Richard's father has no connection with the family business. He's had numerous affairs, some of them quite public, and he has fathered two bastard children." The way she said bastard made it sound less like a curse word and more like the dictionary meaning. "For our close knit family, the whole ordeal was quite scandalous. I think Richard is trying very hard not to get caught up in the same net as his father. But when it comes to women, he is a bit like his father. Women simply adore him."

"Does he have any children?"

"Oh no. He says he doesn't want to be responsible for anything other than himself. At least he knows his limitations, right?"

Renee nodded, wishing she'd talked to Maxi long before she started creating fantasies about Richard.

"Do you have a boyfriend or someone special in your life, Renee?" Maxi exceeded the speed limit, but at least she kept her eyes on the road while she drove.

Renee shook her head.

"Then we should hang out together some time. You can show me all the good places for single women."

"I don't hang out much." Renee pulled her National Celebrity magazine from her purse and flipped through the pages. For now, she needed to put some space between her and the McKinneys. Even the adopted one.

"I've got a lead on several jobs. I'm sure I'll get an offer soon. If I don't, I'm not sure mum and dad will continue to fund me. Richard said if they don't, I could move into one of his spare bedrooms, but I'm sure I'd be cramping his style."

Talking to Maxi was like talking to a puppy. She jumped from subject to subject as if they were playing fetch with the conversation.

"Good luck." Renee's head ached. The sausage from breakfast, the smell of Maxi's cologne, and the long road stretched in front of them weren't getting along together very well. A few moments of quiet might ease the thumping. "If I fall asleep on you, you won't mind will you?"

"Not at all." Maxi reached for the radio dial. "I have music to keep me company." The loud racket of drums and guitars filled the car.

Renee closed her eyes. The horrific music was exactly what she deserved.

Chapter Sixteen

Two months after the wedding and she was just beginning to feel normal. Renee glanced at the time in the corner of her computer. It was well after five. For the second time she was falling asleep in her cubicle. Her eyelids were so heavy she wanted to crawl under the desk and take a nap. Every time she closed her eyes, Richard materialized in her thoughts. Deciphering her feelings for him hadn't been easy. Too bad she didn't know she loved him before she shoved him out of her room in Glen Cove and into the arms of Janie. But talking about love clouded reality.

She turned off the computer and gathered her things. With nothing to do tonight, she'd climb into bed early to get a good night's sleep.

The only McKinney she'd heard from was Egypt. She half expected Richard to try to talk to her, even if she would have ignored him. It was always good to be wanted.

Her cell rang. She fished it from her purse to see Yani's number. "Hey girl."

"Do you know how difficult it is to get the five of us together? I can understand Geeta not being able to come to town. But the rest of us are only two hours apart." She sighed. "We're meeting in Baltimore on Friday. It's halfway for everyone."

"I knew you'd make it happen. Are we staying over?" Renee grabbed her backpack and hurried out of the office.

"No. Trying to find three hours was hard enough. We can't push it. But when we meet, we'll plan something for Memorial Day weekend."

"Okay. I'm getting on the elevator, so I'm probably going to lose you. Text me the name of the restaurant and I'll see you on Friday." She shut off the phone and shoved it back in her purse.

When the elevator reached the ground floor she fell in behind the mass of people exiting the building. With her latest issues of National Celebrity, People and Star it was going to be a good night. The only other thing she needed was some good take-out.

"Hey Renee, what are you doing here?"

Renee turned to find Maxi McKinney running up behind her. She was pretty as ever and as perky as ever. Her natural hair hung in curls around her face. "I work here. What are *you* doing here?"

"I just had a second interview with Gordon and Mann on the third floor. It went well. They said I should hear something by Friday." Her piercing squeal attracted the attention of several people.

"I wish you the best of luck." They walked towards the door together. "Did you receive the thank you gift I sent to you?"

"Yes. But it wasn't necessary. Richard gave me plenty of money to make sure you got home."

Hearing his name made her body stiffen. She wasn't doing as well as she thought at forgetting him. "That was very nice of him. Deep down I think he has a big heart."

Maxi nodded.

"How is Richard doing?"

They stepped outside and moved out of the way of others coming out of the building.

"I guess you haven't heard. Janie claimed to be pregnant. By him." She talked with her hands, excitement danced in her eyes. "Well, it turns out she was lying. He told me he asked her to pee on the stick while he watched. Can you believe she'd do such a thing?"

Renee shook her head. Would anything have turned out different between them if she'd known there was no pregnancy? There was still the drinking. "How did she think she could get away with fooling him? How…how…did he take it?"

"According to him, she said she punched a hole in the condom. He told me she had also tried to break up Declan and Egypt. I think she won't be coming around anymore. I thought she was a nice person. Now I understand why Egypt gave me that lecture the day at the spa. Duh." She paused. "Look, are you free? Maybe we can have a drink," Maxi said.

"I can't tonight." She took a step away from Maxi. Her head was spinning. She was going to be sick. Her lunch was climbing up her throat. "Next week, I promise. I really need to get home." She spun around, running toward the parking lot.

In the safety of her car, she locked the doors and dropped her head against the steering wheel. The last two months had passed in a blur. The only thought occupying space in her head was Richard and getting beyond him.

What should have occupied her mind was her period. When was her last one?

"No. No. No. This can't be happening. It just can't," she said aloud in the car.

By the time she walked into her apartment her heartbeat was so fast she was panting. She dumped the pregnancy tests on the center of the bed. She'd gotten four different brands. Her hands trembled so much that reading the directions was almost impossible.

An hour later she couldn't pee another drop and all the tests were positive. Plastic indicators lined the sink.

Each one shouted at her.

Each one announced its torture.

Each one ripped away a piece of her foundation.

Chapter Seventeen

Renee pulled into the parking garage on Franklin Street. Egypt was the first out of the car, prancing up the walkway before Egypt paid the attendant. Marriage worked for her. Everything about her sparkled as bright as her wedding ring set. Renee had to speed up to catch up to her.

Together they crossed the street to the red awing with the Café Pepe imprinted on it. Morning sickness hadn't been an issue, but the idea of rich Spanish food made her queasy.

"I got a text from Cat. They're already here. Yani and Phoebe rode down with her," Egypt said.

Inside the low ceiling of the restaurant, the smell of garlic and onions was more intense. Renee willed her stomach to cooperate. Since taking the pregnancy test, control over her body seemed limited, like a stranger she needed to get acquainted with.

The receptionist led them through several small rooms before stopping in front of their friends. A blue and white sangria pitcher was already on the table.

"You guys decided not to wait for us, I see." Egypt sat and reached for a glass. After filling it she turned to Renee.

"I think I'll start with water. I am the designated driver." Happy to have an excuse, Renee took a sip from her glass.

Small talk swirled around the table, but Renee was deaf to the conversation. She couldn't hold on to the thread long enough to comment. While her friends' lives steamed straight ahead, hers had stalled. This dinner was supposed to be a happy event. She'd looked forward to it for days. But thoughts of her current situation wouldn't let her enjoy being with them.

They were seated in the restaurant long enough to order appetizers and drinks, when Renee couldn't keep her secret another moment.

"I'm pregnant." Renee didn't mean to blurt the words, but she needed to say them aloud. It was the only way to accept she was carrying Richard's child. She had to get it out there in the universe.

"What?" Egypt's mouth remained opened. "I wasn't gone that long. We talked as soon as I got back. Why are you just telling me?"

"I just found out today, for sure." She pressed her hands in her lap. Something she'd been doing a lot since she found out. "I didn't want to believe those drugstore tests."

"Who is the lucky guy?" Yani asked.

"Nobody special. We've already gone our separate ways." She wanted to sound nonchalant to counteract the churning gathering in her head and heading south, throughout her body. It started the day she looked at the test strips and it hadn't gone away yet.

"Are you sure?" Phoebe chimed in.

"I saw the doctor this morning. I'm sure."

"You don't look happy." Cat had been the quiet one. Renee saw worry in her eyes.

"I'm not. I don't want to be a single mother. I wasn't planning to have a baby."

"Have you at least told the father? Maybe you won't have to do this alone. Maybe he'll want to help you. Maybe the two of you can work things out." If hope was enough, then there was enough of it in Egypt's voice to keep the world afloat.

"No, I haven't. Telling him is a dead end. And that was a lot of maybes."

Cat reached across the table and touched her arm. "Are you going to keep it?"

Renee released the grip on her hands. "I don't know. I don't know what I'm going to do. I haven't had time to think too far ahead, yet."

"You have to keep it. You just have to." Phoebe winced.

"No, I don't, Phoebe. I don't." She didn't mean to snap at Phoebe, but she didn't need the pressure from her either.

“Whatever you decide, you know you can count on us. We’ll be there for you.” Cat’s voice quivered with sincerity. Renee had to look away from the intensity in her eyes.

“Enough. I don’t know what I’m going to do. I haven’t had time to think clearly. Let’s change the conversation for now.” She turned to her friend. “Egypt, did you bring pictures?”

Phoebe sat back in her chair, her hand clasped in defiance. This wasn’t a topic she was going to let go. Renee could tell by the steely look she gave her across the table that she could expect a phone call or visit. But without the facts, Phoebe couldn’t begin to guess the state of confusion she was mired in.

At the end of dinner, Cat, Phoebe, and Yani requested their car from the valet for the drive back to Philly.

Phoebe leaned across the table. “Before you make a decision, please call me. I don’t want you to do something you’ll regret.”

Phoebe meant well. Out of the six of them, she was the most mature. She knew what she wanted to do with her life the moment she came out of the womb. But Renee needed to make the decision that was right for her, without the influence of anyone. To appease her friends, she nodded.

When they were alone, Egypt stared at her for several seconds.

"Are you going to tell me what's going on? I know you, Renee. You didn't have some passing sexual encounter with a faceless guy."

She pressed her tongue to the roof of her mouth. She had to be honest with Egypt. They shared everything and no matter what she decided, she was going to need Egypt's support.

"Richard." Saying his name was difficult. She didn't want to implement him in her predicament. She could see Egypt churning through the options, coming up with a solution Renee wasn't even sure she wanted.

"How…how can that be?" She leaned forward. "I knew you guys didn't just sleep in the apartment." She grinned, thinking she'd solved the riddle.

Renee rolled her eyes. "It didn't happen in D.C., it happened in Glen Cove. It's a long story and please don't make me explain it. We used a condom. We used three of them. I don't know how this happened."

Egypt sat back and sighed. "You have to tell him, Renee. No matter what you decide, he deserves to know." Egypt's face reflected the pain Renee felt.

It wasn't because she didn't want to tell Richard. Every night she dreamed of telling him and the look of joy on his face. But each morning she remembered the tortured expression on his face when he thought Janie was pregnant. The life she imagined included being with a man who wanted to be with her. Not because of a child, but because of love. It sounded dorky, but it's the life she envisioned. The relationship she envisioned was a trillion times better than the one she grew up in. Better than the shouting, the fighting, the drinking that marked her childhood.

"Let me think about it," Renee said.

"I'll go with you if you want."

It was her turn to reach for Egypt's hand. "I've got to do this on my own. No matter what I decide, I'll have to live with the decision."

Chapter Eighteen

The condo should have been big enough. She was the only one living in it. But the loops around the coffee table, then the dining set, then the ottoman near the balcony door wasn't enough space to work out the details of what she needed to do.

Instead of sharing her news with her friends, she should have kept quiet. There was enough racket going on in her head without adding the voices of others.

She spent too much time thinking about the baby. Fear swelled in her chest, making it hard to think about anything else. Everyone had advice, but the only one she valued so far was telling Richard. Keeping this from him would haunt her like a house full of walking dead.

She grabbed her car keys and marched out the door. Growing up in the Payne household took more than gumption and she wasn't a scaredy cat. She could do it.

She was strong.

Determined.

And decisive.

Whatever happened, she could handle it and handle it well. As long as her emotional side didn't take control of her rational thinking, she would be fine. This meeting was going to be calm and matter of fact.

No breaking down.

No crying.

No pleading.

And above all else, no crying. The last thing she needed was pity or for him to think he needed to rescue her.

In her car, she backed out of the parking space. Spring was everywhere. The trees were turning green. Daffodils poked through the soil and promised warmer weather. She was the hibernating bear getting ready to face her future.

The drive to Richard's door blurred into different scenarios and versions of the speech she planned to give him. She wasn't asking him for anything, only giving him information. He didn't have to accept it. He only needed to hear it.

She stood outside of his sprawling home. A man who didn't want marriage or children, or commitment, didn't need a house that screamed all of the above. For a McKinney to live in a modest domicile was probably forbidden. She rang the doorbell and waited, taking shallow breaths to shore up her resolve that was suddenly non-existent. Maybe she should have run a comb through her hair and changed out of her jeans, but her appearance didn't seem important when she rushed out of the house. Only there, coming face to face with the man she couldn't stop thinking about, did it seem important.

He snatched open the door. Seeing his dark tousled hair and dark eyes was a startling reminder of everything she missed. Richard was off limits. They lived in different worlds. He couldn't live in her world with her no drinking policy and she couldn't live in his with the drinking, partying, and women. The earth could have shook and she wouldn't have felt anything more than the tumbling going on in her stomach.

"Renee." He looked beyond her as if he was expecting someone else. "What are you doing here?" His question wasn't asked in a derogatory manner, it was more of a surprise. "Please come in, come in." He stepped aside allowing her inside, then closed the door.

With his hands behind his back, he looked down at her. He was happy to see her, she could tell from the gleam in his eyes. "I didn't think I'd ever see you again, unless Declan and Egypt invited us all together to celebrate something awesome, again. But it's always good to see you. I take it you're not still enraged at me for my behavior?"

"No. I'm not. And maybe I had no right to be mad at you back then. It's just you have some stuff going on that makes me uncomfortable. Obviously you must have worked it all out, you look great."

"I haven't had a drink since that awful night, thanks to your response. And, I'm not going to be a daddy. So, yes, I'm exceptional. But, I get the impression you didn't come way out here to check on me. Even though I wish you had."

"Uh, I was hoping we could sit down and talk." She stopped. "Did I catch you at a bad time? We can do this later. Maybe I should have called you first." She fumbled through the thoughts pushing for attention in her head.

"No, not at all." He gave her an appreciative look, lingering on her breasts for longer than a moment. "You look stunning, Renee. I've missed you."

"After I've had my say you might not feel the same way."

"Okay. We can sit here in my office." He gestured across the hall to a room she would have called a library. There were books on three of the four walls. One bookcase was covered in leather-bound books. He chose not to sit behind his desk but instead gestured toward the sofa where they both sat.

"I'm glad you're here." He gave her a tender smile. "It's really good to see you."

She looked up into his eyes. "This isn't easy, so I'm just going to say it. Even if it doesn't sound right."

He nodded. “Okay.” He placed his hand on her knee. The expression was more intimate than she needed. She wanted to pull away, but she wanted to get through her speech, then she’d focus on other stuff.

“I’m pregnant.” Getting the words out left her exhausted. She fell back against the sofa and inhaled. His face changed, like someone had punched him in the gut. His face went from rosy to colorless.

“Is this a joke? If it is, I’m not finding it very funny.” He removed his hand from her knee and pushed back into the corner.

“It’s not contagious. And no, this is not a joke.”

He jumped off the sofa, backing away from her. “Are you certain?”

“I took four pregnancy tests and my doctor confirmed it last week. I’m not sure what I’m going to do yet about the baby, but I thought it was important for me to tell you. I think you deserve to know. I stopped by just to inform you. I’m not expecting anything more.”

“Janie wasn’t pregnant. It was all a ruse. Another one of her great inventions, this time she intended to drag me under.” He turned around, walking behind his desk.

She jumped up. “Well, I wanted you to know. I think I’d better go now.”

"Ummmm." He placed his hand at the back of his neck. "You can't dump such life changing news on me and walk out. What am I supposed to do?"

"Nothing. Nothing at all. Like I said, I'm not asking you for anything. Really, I'm not. I just thought you ought to know. I don't want money. I don't want your time. I don't want you to marry me." Her eyes stung. In a moment she was going to start to cry. Damn it.

He smacked his forehead. "Wait right there. Please don't move." Before she could respond, he dashed out of the room. She heard his footsteps on the stairs.

She shook her hands, trying to loosen the tension taking over her body. She faced the window overlooking the front lawn and swiped at her eyes. He was not going to see her cry. No matter what, she would be tough and fight the extra hormones that wanted to control her body.

She examined the room. His desk had one picture frame on it. Who was the one person important enough to hold such a special place? She picked up the frame and flipped it around to see the picture.

Baffled by the image, she shook her head. Then she recognized it. It was the picture he'd taken with his cell phone of her in New York, the one with the sheet over her head. She recognized the room décor.

At the sound of him running back down the stairs, she placed the frame back in position on the desk and braced herself. Ten thousands volts of electricity traveled through her body, jolting every crucial organ. Why did he have her picture on his desk? Even if her face wasn't visible, it was still her.

He was winded when he came back into the office and placed a blue box of Trojans on the desk. The color was back in his face along with wild-eyed excitement.

"Why do you have that picture on your desk?" She picked it up and held it out to him.

"Because I liked it."

"But—"

He removed it from her hand and put it back on the desk. "You said I could keep it since no one could see your face." His cheeks darkened and he looked away.

She focused her attention on the condom box. Was he implying he wasn't the father because they'd used condoms? Her heartbeat accelerated, bucking against her ribs like a runaway bull.

"Look, Richard. I know we used a condom. And I know Janie lied to you. But I'm telling the truth." She reached for her purse. "I don't need this. If you don't believe me, that's fine. I've got to go." She tried to rush pass him.

"No. Just give me a minute." He opened the box and dangled a roll of condoms from his right hand.

She placed her hand on her hip. "Oh, you're really funny. Since I'm pregnant you think I'll jump in the sack with you. What are you thinking, you can't do any more harm?" Her voice was so high she almost didn't recognize it. She had agonized over telling him, wondering if it was the right thing, trying to make a decision she could live with, and he wanted to make jokes.

"No, no." He pulled her toward the window. With the condoms held up to the light, he closed one eye. "She said she punched holes in the condoms. Janie, she—"

"Are you kidding me?" She stood closer to him, angling her head right and left to get a better look. Squinting with one eye to examine the row of condoms. "Would she have pierced the whole box? I don't see anything."

"To improve her odds, she would have pierced her parents. The woman is certifiably crazy." He put his face closer to the foil wrappers. "Look! There is a hole." He used his index finger to point to it. "All of these have a hole in them." He trailed his finger down the foil packs. "All of them."

She nudged him aside to get a better look. "I see them, now. There and there." Her stomach squeezed around the bundle forming in her belly. She flopped on the sofa. Suddenly she didn't have the strength to stand up. The holes could have been in her soul because everything holding her up leaked out.

He sat beside her and for several minutes neither of them spoke. She stared at him unable to find anything appropriate to say. How do you tell someone they crapped on your life?

"How could this happen? She was supposed to get pregnant. Not me. This was between you and her. I wasn't supposed to be dragged into it."

"I'm so sorry, Renee. It never occurred to me she would have punched holes in the whole box. I didn't think she was capable of such deviant behavior." He shook his head.

Tears filled her eyes. "I promised myself I wasn't going to cry. I was going to handle this like a business meeting. But, but, I can't." A sob escaped from her throat. "Getting pregnant like normal people I can accept, but this, I can't…I can't…"

He gathered her in his arms and rocked her. Snuggled next to him was a wonderful feeling. To have that moment regularly would have been marvelous. Imagining people who did made her shiver. Something this comforting shouldn't be limited to only those lucky enough to find a mate. Her heart ached with emptiness.

His hold was soothing, but it would take more than a kind gesture to calm her. To get sucked into the drama between Richard and Janie was beyond cruel.

Striking out at someone or something wouldn't ease the turbulence taking over her body.

"Renee, please don't cry. We'll handle this." He continued to rock her, increasing the speed as if it would improve her state of mind.

Her nose dripped on his shirt. "Please give me a tissue."

"Are you going to be okay if I leave you?" He didn't release her.

She nodded.

He left the room but was back within seconds, handing her a fistful of tissues. She had to look a hot mess, but her appearance wasn't important. She expected him to be upset or to see a flash of anger, about her news, but he seemed calm. Too calm.

"Thanks to Janie's handiwork, there could be other women out there having your baby. Why aren't you upset?" she demanded to know.

"I think you're upset enough for the both of us. Besides, I haven't been with anyone since you." He dropped his head.

She closed her eyes and tried to slow her breathing. "Isn't that wonderful for you." She used the tissue to wipe her eyes. "But now I'm more uncertain about everything than I was before. How can I keep this baby?"

He jumped off the sofa. The look he threw at her made her cringe.

Chapter Nineteen

He walked the length of the sofa, looking down at her. Judgment filled his eyes. Maybe it was the cavalier way she'd announced her indecision, but she wanted to sound convincing. She was painted in a corner, looking at a future that was too cloudy to see the resolution, and pregnant by a man who didn't care for her.

"Don't I have some say?" Richard's words were underscored with accusation. He increased his strides, putting more distance between them.

She stood, too. At least this way she didn't feel like a child being scolded. "You can say anything you want. But you know this is my decision." She waited for him to agree. When he didn't, she repeated herself.

With him on one side of the room and her on the other, he squared off. "I can't begin to imagine how upset you must be. But I think I need to be a part of this decision. A baby isn't the end of the world. It's not like you've been diagnosed with a fatal disease."

This discussion wasn't going how she'd expected. He should have been relieved she wasn't demanding money, or marriage. Nothing would change in his life.

"Listen to me. I'm not trying to tie you down. I don't want anything from you. Nothing."

"You're having my baby, so everything changes." His voice was calm, but it was lined with determination that exuded authority.

"Okay." She reached for her purse, refusing to be intimidated into a decision. "I don't think we're going to resolve anything today. I need to give you some time to mull this over. After a few days when the emotion has worn off you'll see this differently."

"I don't think I will. I want the baby."

She ran her hand over her ponytail, smoothing it down. He wanted the baby, but not her. Her head pounded, like it was splitting in two. "Richard, I can't do this. I'm not prepared to have this conversation."

He grabbed her arm, halting her rush for the door. "You must promise me you won't do anything until we talk again."

She stared into his eyes. "Where is this coming from? In Glen Cove you went on and on about not wanting to be with anyone. Not being like your father. A child needs parents, two of them to love him and help walk him through this world."

"This baby will have two parents. You and me." He pointed at her, then back to himself.

She shook her head. “Two people don’t make two parents.” She wrenched her arm away from him. “I’ve really got to go.”

“Renee,” he yelled her name. “Promise me you won’t do anything until we talk again. You can at least do that, can’t you? What difference will a day or two make?”

She could have stayed and gazed into his eyes for days hoping to find he was willing to return the love she had for him. His eyes were intense with promise. But she had a pocket full of broken promises. The tug on her heart pressed her to trust him. A day or two wouldn’t turn her to stone, but it would come close. “Okay,” she said with reluctance. “But only because I need time to think and sort this out, not because you’re demanding it.”

He released a visible sigh of relief.

Before he asked for something else she wasn’t sure she could give, she raced out the door and to her car. The sun had set. The air was cooler. She shivered. Even when she turned the heat on in the car she continued to shake. It had less to do with the temperature and more to do with the meeting with Richard. What could he possibly be thinking? A baby was a lifetime commitment, not a whimsical venture they could turn away from when the thrill faded. Even if she decided to keep the baby, she didn’t want to be tied to a man who didn’t love her, cherish her, and want her. The world she knew and controlled was spinning away from her. She knew the feeling. She hated it.

Chapter Twenty

Sleeping on the sofa overnight was not a good idea. With the shade still closed the gloomy room matched her disposition. Her body felt sore and knotted. But it's where she'd ended up when she returned from Richard's. There hadn't been a lot of arguing, or shouting or anger. The two of them had behaved like real grown-ups.

The ringing phone pulled her away from her thoughts. She pushed the magazines out of her lap and picked up the receiver.

"Have you talked to him yet?" Egypt bypassed the preliminaries and cut straight to the point of her call.

Renee straightened out her legs. "Yes. Yesterday."

"Don't make me drag it out of you. How did it go?"

"Not at all like I imagined." She shared the conversation with Egypt.

"Now what?"

"Egypt, I feel like I'm being pushed through a meat grinder. I promised not to do anything until we talked again. I've never been so perplexed about anything before. I've only known a week and already I'm starting to have feelings for this baby. I've been rubbing my stomach and it's still flat. But Richard is making it more complicated. I can see myself loving and raising this baby, but I can't see the two of us doing this together."

"You know you can count on me. I'd be there for you."

"I know and thank you. But this has got to be a decision I make alone. Not because of Richard, or my sisters, or the dirty looks from Phoebe."

"Everybody has an opinion, Renee. But the only opinion that matters in this situation is what's right for you. I'll stand by you."

"Am I being selfish to think I can raise this baby alone? I have a full time job which is demanding. Sure I can financially provide for a child, but I'd have to find a daycare or hire a nanny. There wouldn't be a regular father figure. I think I'm not being fair."

"Renee, you would make a good mother. Don't question your abilities. Between all of us, the baby will have plenty of godmothers and godfathers. It sounds like you're coming to a decision."

"I think I am."

They hung up and Renee burrowed into the sofa. Thoughts fast-forwarded through her head so quickly, she couldn't grab one of them. One minute she was decorating a nursery, the next minute she was pushing a stroller through Rock Creek Park.

The intercom buzzed, but she couldn't release her hold on the sofa to see who it was. She wasn't expecting anyone or anything.

When the noise stopped, she remained on the sofa in the silence. The quiet didn't last long. Her cell phone began to vibrate. She picked it up from the table. Richard's number glowed in the dim room.

"Hello." Her voice was as flat as her back was on the couch. Any other time she would have been ecstatic to hear from him, but not this time.

"Can I come up?" he asked.

"You're here? I thought we'd set a time to get together." She swung her feet off the sofa and sat straight.

"Okay, let me up and we can start scheduling."

She allowed him up, then rushed to the bathroom to brush her teeth and straighten out her ponytail. Her makeup was smeared. She only had time to clean the mascara from under her eyes.

He rang the doorbell before she had time to change, so he'd get a second viewing of the same clothes she wore yesterday. Only now they were wrinkled.

She opened the door for him and returned to the sofa to neaten the huge pile of magazines. He entered the apartment. She couldn't help but notice he hadn't shaved. The stubble on his face wasn't thick, but it certainly was sexy. Thoughts like that had landed her in trouble. She had to think with her brain and not her heart.

"Just because I'm having your baby doesn't mean you can pop in any time you want to." Her tone was severe, but she needed to protect herself from him. Richard had enough charm to make her do silly things, like sleep with him, believe in him and have a baby for him.

"It's good to know now that you're in the family way it hasn't dulled your sharp tongue. But don't you think you should watch how you talk in front of the baby?"

She cut him a sharp look. Wanting to counter his question with an edgy retort, but she couldn't. She wanted to fall into his arms and be held. To be told everything was going to work out just fine.

She gave his comment a dismissive wave.

"I've never had a woman be so direct with me. It's kind of refreshing" He stared down at her.

"I've never had a man as arrogant as you. I don't like it. You enjoy telling people what to do and expect it to be done on your timing, don't you?"

"Okay, that's enough for this critique session." He kissed her forehead.

"What's in the bag?"

"I'm going to cook dinner for us. It's a good thing. You look like you could use some TLC. Aren't those the same clothes you wore yesterday?"

"As a matter of fact they are. I've had more important things to think about than my wardrobe."

"Why is it so dark in here? It's a beautiful day and it's past noon." He opened the blinds, flooding the room with light.

She shielded her eyes against the glare. "Who told you, you could open my blinds?"

He continued into the kitchen, placed the bags on the counter, and then directed his attention to her. "*We* have important things to think about." He stood in the archway. His body was rigid.

From the set of his shoulders he was all business. Sure it would be wonderful to share her fears and joys with him, but he had his agenda and she had hers. She could bait him into an argument, but it took too much stamina.

In all her adult life no man had ever come to her home and cooked for her. They had been willing to take her out, or order in, but never had anyone gone through the steps of cooking a meal. Either her hormones were beginning to change or she was touched by his gesture. Her eyes stung, threatening to spill tears like a faucet.

She inhaled a deep breath and stood. "What's for dinner? Can you even cook?" She strolled into the kitchen to glance over his shoulder.

“Fish and chips of course. It’s easy and quick. And you’re gonna love it.” He took the ingredients, placing them on the counter. Then he whipped out a magazine and with a flourish handed it to her.

“What is this?”

“I know you have an obsession for celeb magazines, so I thought you’d get a kick from a British rag. You may not know all the stars, but you might find it interesting.”

She accepted it. “That was very thoughtful of you. When did you…never mind.” She scratched her head. “You know, I give up trying to figure you out.”

“Good, it’s not easy keeping you on your toes. Why don’t you sit there and keep me company.” He pointed to the chair, and continued to point until she sat down. Once she was seated, he turned his back and began the food preparation.

“How have you been feeling? Any morning sickness?” He rinsed the fish and placed it on a paper towel.

“I didn’t even know I was pregnant until last week. So anytime I was uncomfortable I thought it was something I ate or the way I slept. Now I’ll pay more attention.”

“Do you have any diet restrictions? I know alcohol is out, but are there others?” He maneuvered around the kitchen like an expert.

She responded to his questions and watched as he cut the potatoes using his own knife. This visit was planned. Who travels with their own knife?

"When are you due?" There was a casualness to his tone, but it was lined with something more. Maybe it was concern.

"In November. I didn't know this was going to be an inquisition."

"I'm just trying to get caught up. Which way are you leaning? More towards keeping it or—"

"You know I don't understand you. In New York you went on and on about not wanting to settle down, not being good with commitment. I think you said something about rather having a dog. You're the man who's so sexually active you keep a box of condoms. A whole box."

He turned. The smile he gave her was wide. His whole face lit up. "I said I was good with babies and dogs. At the time I was thinking of other people's babies, but I'm certain the statement applies to babies of my own, too."

"Don't you think children need a mom and a dad?"

He dropped the potatoes into hot oil. "I do. And our child will have a mom and a dad." The sizzle made it almost difficult to hear him. "My father has two children outside of his marriage to my mom. All he does is write checks. I've never wanted to be anything like my father. In fact, I'm sure I'll be a wonderful dad. It's the only thing I've thought about since you told me."

"You didn't seem too happy when you thought Janie was pregnant."

His smile disappeared, fading into a sour expression. "That's different. Very different. I don't feel anything for Janie."

Her heart began to race, taking off like a wild stallion. What was he implying? She rose from the chair. In the kitchen she positioned herself to see his face. She needed to make sure she understood what he was saying. "What does that mean, Richard?"

He put down the knife and faced her. "I care for you, Renee. Very much."

"I see." She fell back against the wall. Her brain fought with her tongue over how to respond. The room began to spin. She was going to fall.

Richard caught her before her knees gave out. He carried her to the sofa.

"Are you okay? Should I call the doctor?" His words ran together.

"I'm fine. I just got warm. Give me a minute."

He peered at her for several seconds before going back into the kitchen. She could hear him from her position on the sofa. She closed her eyes and tried to imagine a life like this. One where she could depend on someone to be there when she needed them. Someone to cook a meal for her when she was hungry. Someone to share her unadventurous days with. Never had she wanted someone more than she did in that moment.

She opened her eyes and changed her position to be able to see him.

He checked the fish. The golden brown fillets made her stomach growl. The only thing she'd eaten all day was several handfuls of almonds. After putting it on paper towels, he pulled plates from the cabinet.

"Dinner is ready. Do you think you can eat?" He carried the food to the table, then returned to the kitchen and searched the refrigerator. "What have you got to drink?"

"There's carbonated water. I ditched all the sugary drinks."

"Good idea. You're doing all the right stuff." He returned with two bottles.

"Have you told anyone?" He served up the fish and chips, filling her plate.

"Everyone knows and everyone has an opinion."

"I'm a little disappointed I'm the last one you told." He stared at her across the table. "Tell me what I need to say to convince you to keep the baby. I know you don't want my money or me, but there must be something that you need to help you make a decision."

It was hard to speak. Were there words to set this conversation on the right course? She wanted him, more than he knew and more than she should.

No matter how hard she tried to erase him from her life, he kept coming back. Now, with a baby, he would become a permanent fixture.

"I don't know how to answer your question. If the answer were as easy as you make it sound then I would have made a decision a week ago."

He nodded several times and continued to look into her eyes. "Fair enough. How about we just enjoy dinner for now?"

The interrogation ended long enough for her to enjoy the meal he prepared especially for her. The condo was quiet, the lights were dim with the sun fading from the sky, and the food was good. This was the most perfect date she'd had in a long time and it wasn't really a date.

"You're staring at me," Richard said.

"I'm sorry. I was thinking. It was very nice of you to cook for me. I don't like to cook and I haven't eaten much today."

Alarm flared in his eyes.

"Calm down. I'm going to do better. I know nutrition is important, but after our discussion yesterday I was upset, so I came home and crashed on the sofa."

"I didn't mean to upset you. When I want something, I tend to bulldoze my way through until I get it." He put his fork down. "You're right to weigh this out carefully. But for me, the decision was made when you became pregnant. It was fate. It was meant to be."

They were silent for a moment. He pushed his plate to the middle of the table and stared at her for several moments.

"Maxi told me she saw you. She now has a job in your building," he said.

"Oh great," Egypt said, even though she didn't think it was going to be wonderful seeing a constant reminder of Richard on a regular basis. "She told me about Janie and the pregnancy hoax."

"Yes, our Maxi is quite the talker. She's not very good at keeping confidences. If you have a secret, don't share it with her," he chuckled, but from the look on his face he meant every word.

"I hope you won't tell her I'm the one who actually got pregnant from Janie's little stunt. The whole idea would be funny if it weren't so unfortunate."

"No, I won't tell her, or anyone else for that matter until we've worked through this."

She wanted to reach across the table and touch some part of him. His hand, his shoulder, his lips. But the intimacy they'd share at the wedding had vanished. He almost felt like a stranger.

"I've missed you, Renee."

Her first impression was to debunk his statement. But the tenderness in his eyes made it impossible. She couldn't decipher what was real and what was for show. She wanted to believe it all.

"You didn't call me or try to get in touch with me after you dashed out of Glen Cove."

"You told me not to. You made your decision very clear," he said.

"I was upset. Janie was at the spa earlier in the day. She said she was there to claim you, or something close to those words. Then you told me she was having your baby, and you were drinking. It was too much." She lowered her head as the memory threatened to overtake her.

He leaned closer to her. "Which upset you the most, Janie being pregnant or my taking a drink?" His question gave her nowhere to run, nothing quirky to say to defuse the familiarity bubbling between them.

"I…I—"

"You have to pick one and you have to tell me the truth."

"Okay, it was the drinking. I know the damage unchecked drinking can do. I don't have any experience with babies and baby-mommy-drama, so I didn't find that as frightening."

He nodded as if he understood her dilemma. "Cute. But I don't do drama."

She put up her index finger. "That's what you say, but since I've met you it's been one big drama palooza. First you almost broke up Declan and Egypt, then getting you to Glen Cove without allowing you to drink, then the seduction in my room in New York and then the icing on the cake." She pointed at her belly. "Drammmmma."

He tilted his head just enough for the dining room light to catch the sharp angle of his chin. "You want promises, assurances, but life doesn't always come wrapped in a pretty pink bow. Sometimes you've got to have faith. When it comes to relationships, you give it everything you've got and you pray it works out. Don't you think everyone is a little fearful of putting their self out there?"

"How long have you been practicing your speech? And do you buy that mumbo-jumbo?"

His seldom seen smile lit up his face. "You are very charming. I think I could listen to you talk all night."

"If that's your way of asking can you spend the night, the answer is no."

He used his foot to pull her chair next to his. Before she could protest, he pressed his mouth to hers and slipped in his tongue. If she weren't sitting down, her legs would have given out on her, again. His closeness made it hard to think of reasons why she should pull away. She wrapped her hands around his neck and deepened the kiss. Being able to kiss him was magical, the kind of stuff that filled her dreams.

The passion between them grew more intense. All the emotions she'd tried to ignore surfaced with a vengeance, leaving her unable to fight.

His hands touched her neck, her shoulders and her back. But through her clothes she was being shortchanged. Just as the thought ran through her head, he grabbed her hand and led her to the bedroom.

He unzipped her sweater and pushed it off her shoulders. After kissing each one he unhooked her bra, finally freeing her tender breasts. He cupped each one with affection. Maybe he sensed the difference in them. He traced his tongue around her nipples.

"I've dreamed about making love to you, again. I didn't think it was ever going to be possible." He helped her remove the rest of her clothes. When she was naked he stood back, his eyes graced every inch of her body. Unhurried, he lingered on her breasts. "You have a beautiful body. I don't think I could ever get enough of it."

She took two steps toward him and unbuttoned his shirt. The process took longer because he stopped her after every button to plant a kiss on her lips. She took all the time she needed to enjoy his body. His shaft was warm and throbbed in the palm of her hand. She held him firm, stroking his penis until he groaned her name.

"Renee, please stop."

With no promises of tomorrow, she may not have another opportunity. With his clothes in a pile on the floor next to hers, she studied his body. Trying to remember the nuances that made him the man she loved.

“I can’t wait another moment.” He captured her mouth and maneuvered her to the bed. This time he shoved the magazines to the floor.

He climbed on top of her, pressing her into the mattress. She folded her arms around him. This was exactly what she imagined for them. Lovemaking so steamy she couldn’t be reasonable. For a few hours she wanted someone else to handle the responsibility for everything piled on her shoulders. For a few moments, she didn’t want to be tough or worried about the future. The force field insulating her from disappointment evaporated, she felt her body grow lighter.

He eased into her. The sensation was more exquisite than anything she’d ever felt. Their time in Glen Cove was wonderful, but this time was better. She wished she could open up to him, to stop hiding her feelings. But that kind of exposure could be harmful.

“I love you.” She snapped her mouth shut. Where did those words come from? How could she be so foolish? In twenty-seven years she’d never said those words to a man. Never. Did being pregnant disconnect her brain from her common sense? Maybe he didn’t hear her. Maybe he’d be kind enough to ignore her if he did.

He slowed his movement, pushed up on his palms and looked down at her. “If you love me, why don’t you include me in on what’s going on? Why are you trying so hard to push me away?”

She tightened her legs around him, hoping to distract him. “Can we talk about this later?”

“No, I want to talk about it now.” He continued to move within her. “When you’re vulnerable you’re honest.”

“A relationship takes two people, Richard.”

He pushed deeper into her and held eye contact. “I’ve told so many women I loved them when I didn’t, I didn’t want to do the same thing with you. I’ve tried to show you how much you mean to me.” He rotated his hips slowly.

“I need to hear the words.”

“I adore you, Renee.” He eased in and out of her body, his movements strong and steady. “I’ve thought about you day and night since leaving Glen Cove.” He paused for a moment. His gaze grew more earnest. She was awash in emotion, absorbing every word.

“I need you, Renee.” He pushed deeper. His warmth surrounded her. The confines holding her down loosened and she flew into ecstasy head on.

Without breaking eye contact, his body went rigid. With a final thrust he shuddered with an abandonment she’d never seen before. “I love you, Renee.”

Richard collapsed on top of her. His breathing was as heavy as hers. Together they sounded like they'd just scaled Mount Kilimanjaro. Her heart was lying open to him. Her exposure was daunting. This was the test she'd never wanted to take, having to choose between love and the unknown.

"You didn't have to say you loved me. I want to keep the baby, no matter what your feelings are." She heard the ultra-sensitiveness in her voice.

He sighed loud enough for her to hear before rolling onto the bed. With his hands cupped on each side of her face, he kissed her long and deep.

"Love, I'm not sure what I can say to you to let you know my intentions are honorable. I have no desire to mislead you or pretend something for the sake of a child. My parents lived a pretend life and I can tell you it's no advantage for a baby." He tugged her chin and looked into her eyes. "I think you're looking for an iron-clad money back guarantee. But life doesn't offer them. Love is a risk, you've got to be willing to risk something to get the benefit."

"So now what do we do?" Emotion blocked her throat so her question came out as a whisper.

"Whatever we damn well please. How about I do you again?" His penis pressed against her thigh.

"You've got yourself a deal." She climbed on top of him.

****

Renee glanced over and looked at the clock. It was after midnight. Richard lay beside her, his hand on her stomach. She tried to recall every word and promise he'd made since showing up at her door. There were too many to recall. In their sexual bliss, how much of it would hold up in the morning light?

She walked her fingers down his chest. "Richard you've got to wake up and go home."

"Why?" he asked without hesitating.

"I thought you were asleep," she said.

"I haven't slept since you told me I was going to be a father." He spoke without opening his eyes. "Why do I have to go home?"

"We need a little time. Let's see if we feel the same way tomorrow evening. About each other, not the baby. The baby I'm sure about."

He used his elbows and sat up in the bed. "I have no doubt about my feelings, but if you need time—" He kissed her forehead. "I understand."

He swung his legs off the bed and stretched. "Tomorrow, I'm taking you on a proper date. I'll pick you up at seven."

"I'll be ready." She watched him dress, not really wanting him to go, but she needed a little space to sort things out. Some of it still felt impossible, and too close to make-believe.

When he was fully clothed, he kissed her again, this time with more passion.

"Hey, Richard," she said before he left the bedroom. "Thank you."

From the doorway he turned to her. "*Thank you*, love.

Chapter Twenty-One

Renee checked her appearance in the mirror one final time. She wanted to look better than she had when he'd arrived yesterday. It was pretty easy to accomplish. She'd rejected the black dress as too severe, and opted to wear a sleeveless lavender sheath with a plunging neckline that showed off her new assets. The ponytail was gone, replaced with a sleek straight style that was more elegant. Her heart continued to beat faster than normal. So much was happening so fast, but she didn't want to slow down, afraid it might evaporate under close scrutiny.

The intercom rang at six-fifty. Her Prince Charming was early. Before dashing to answer it she closed her eyes for a moment to murmur a prayer. Let him be the same man who walked out her door in the early morning hours. A girlfriend and a baby was a lot to sign up for all at once. He might have gotten buyer's remorse.

She gave the okay for the doorman to let him up, and walked the length of the living room while she waited. There was one good reason not to love Richard—the drinking—but too many good ones to turn her heart away. Life was about taking chances and she was ready to take a big one, on him.

He knocked at the door.

"It's open." She stood in the middle of the room, holding her hands in front of her.

He stepped in and stopped. He wore a black suit, white shirt, and gold paisley tie. His shoes looked freshly polished. For several moments he stared intently at her and she couldn't tear her eyes off him. Her heart thundered in her chest.

"I don't think I've ever seen you look more beautiful," he said.

"You look quite dashing yourself."

He crossed the room and gathered her in his arms. His kiss hadn't lost any of its fervor from earlier.

"I know you have some reservations about my drinking. I still contend it's not an issue. But you are more important to me than anything. For you, I promise I'll never take another drink. I know you were worried about me having a box of condoms, also. I don't think I'll have a need for a condom. A box or otherwise."

"It's too early to make those kinds of promises. I think we need more time. We need to date for a while," she said.

"I'm done with dating. I don't need another minute. I want to be with you." He dropped down on one knee and pulled a velvet box from his pocket.

"What are you doing down there? Have you lost your mind?" She swatted his shoulder.

"Oh no. I'm not asking you to marry me. Not yet, anyway." With a snap of his thumb he popped the box open. "It's a chocolate diamond. It almost matches your complexion. It's a promise ring. I promise to be faithful. I promise not to drink. And I promise I'll always love you."

"Please get up. In the States, you only get down on one knee when you're proposing." She extended her hand to help him up.

"I want you to take me serious. As serious as I am." The glint in his eyes matched the sincerity of his words.

"I wasn't expecting…I don't know…I don't know what to say." She pushed back the tears.

"Say yes. Say you're willing to give us a chance." He lifted her chin.

"Yes. I think we deserve a chance." She pressed up on her toes and kissed him.

JOIN THE JACKI KELLY NEWSLETTER at Jackikelly.com!

So you can stay tuned to new releases, appearance and events and prizes. She's away giving away something.

ABOUT THE AUTHOR

Jacki Kelly has written dozens of short stories and several books. She lives in the North East with her husband and one loveable dog. She loves hearing from her readers so please contact her.

Connect with her online:
http://www.jackikelly.com
Twitter - @jackikellybooks
http://facebook.com/jackikellyauthor

If you enjoyed reading Done With Dating, please tell everyone you know. Please post a review for other readers on your favorite reading forum.

DONE WITH DATING

Jacki Kelly

Smashwords Edition
ISBN: 978-1-9422202-08-0
First Edition Electronic January 2016
Published by Yobachi Publishing, LLC

This is a book of fiction. Names, characters, places and incidents either are the product of the author's imagination or are used fictitiously. Any resemblance to actual persons, living or dead or events or locales is entirely coincidental.